PRESSURE

PRESSURE

A MEMOIR

ERIC CANORI

PEERLESS DEVELOPMENT

PEERLESS DEVELOPMENT

An imprint of Peerless Development, LLC

This book may be purchased in bulk at special discounts for sales promotion, corporate gifts, fund-raising, or educational purposes. For details, please send inquiries to:

info@ericcanori.com

Library of Congress Cataloging-in-Publication Data has been applied for.

Paperback ISBN: 979-8-9856447-0-8

Ebook ISBN: 979-8-9856447-1-5

CONTENTS

AUTHOR'S NOTE

In this memoir, I have recreated events and experiences from my memories of them. In order to maintain anonymity of some individuals, I have changed names and certain identifying details. Conversations in the book are not word-for-word transcripts. Instead, I've written them in a way that captures the real emotion and the real meaning of what was said, without the loss of the essential truthfulness of the exchanges.

PROLOGUE

I t was a cold day in November 2008, I was twenty-nine years old, and considered by many to be an adventure seeker. I liked fast cars, intelligent women, good vibes, summer campfires, Hollywood parties, and escape plans. I also liked cash, and I had more than I could count. I had already invested in the film industry, the ski industry, the real estate industry, and most notably, the precious metal industry. I suppose you could say I was very good at scattering money. To be more precise, "scatter hoarding" my money, the same way a squirrel buries food in multiple locations to protect it from a related species. The only difference was I buried millions of dollars of gold in various locations to protect it from the government, and today I was at one of those locations, doing just that: burying $2 million worth of gold bars deep in my mom's backyard.

The hole I was digging for my cache was about three feet wide and already knee deep. I had a firm grip on the wooden shaft of the pointed shovel, and my full-grain leather hiking boots were smashing down on its kickplate. No one could see me, because my mom's yard was surrounded by woods; only the neighboring wildlife sensed I was there. I'm not even sure I knew I was there, because by now I had been operating like a ghost for well over a decade and I felt invisible. I also felt pain, but within that pain—I found freedom.

This memoir is a steady drip of escalating action, all the way up to where I go head-to-head with the United States government. You will not only learn about my pains, fears, and adventures, but by the end of this book you'll see that you can get anything you want in life, because like me, you were hardwired to win.

1

GROUNDED

I t was 1993. I was fourteen, grounded as usual, and I found myself sitting on my bedroom floor with the bass line from the Rolling Stones' "Sympathy for the Devil" thumping beneath me. The music was coming from my mom's regular weekend party downstairs, which I assumed would go late into the night, because they usually did. Sometimes I'd wake up at 5 a.m. to the sound of a glass breaking, someone vomiting, or a table being knocked over.

Mom wanted me to be studying, but since I couldn't focus, I shoved my history book to the side, placed my yearbook on the carpet in front of me, and opened it. It wasn't full of signatures or glorious memories, but it did have a beautiful picture in it that I looked at often. Her name was Jaime, and she sat behind me in French class. She had nice curves, a pretty face, and long, silky black hair. I wanted a girl like her, but I didn't have a chance, because when I flipped the page, there was Alex, on homecoming court, regularly recognized for outstanding athletic performance. He always had the newest sneakers, the trendiest attire, extra lunch money in his pocket, and about six girlfriends—Jaime being one. I often thought if I could be like

Alex, I might have a chance, but I was out of his league and more like my lone wolf buddy, Kyle: quiet, timid, and reserved.

As the party below progressed, I cracked open my bedroom door, inched my way out onto the large balcony, and leaned over the railing, gazing into the foyer of our modern contemporary home. In any direction I looked, I could see oversized windows, cathedral ceilings, and skylights. Our house was surprisingly impressive, considering our knockoff clothes and refrigerator full of rationed food items from the Sunday flyer.

I knew the party had moved to the back porch, because all I could hear was high-pitched drunken laughter and gibbered half-sentences filtering into the house from a distance, which is what I'd been waiting to hear all week, because this meant I could finally sneak into Mom's bedroom.

I could see the door to Mom's room, down off the landing of the split-level staircase, and once I made it there, I walked in, grabbed the VHS tape I wanted, inserted it into the VCR, and hit play. Because when Mom had her party, I had mine—all alone in her bedroom with *Miami Vice*—a show with guns, girls, boats, and chase scenes. And Don Johnson, the slickest guy I'd ever seen. He lived on a sailboat, drove a Ferrari, and wore white linen suits with tropical shirts. He always had a beautiful woman on his arm. In fact, all the wealthy guys in the show did, and this made me think money was the key to attracting women. It made sense, because all the rich kids in school always had girls swarming around them, too. Plus, Mom constantly complained about not having enough money, so in my mind, women gravitated toward confident guys with money.

After the DEA used a wired informant to take down a cocaine dealer, the show ended, and I returned the tape to its rightful place before making my way to the kitchen for some water.

While filling my glass at the kitchen sink, I could see Mom

out of the corner of my eye wobbling on the porch as she fumbled with the screen door. When she eventually managed to slide it open, she noticed me and said: "Oh . . . hi, Eric. Have you been studying?"

"I have; it's going well," I answered.

"Well, come outside and say 'hi' to everyone," she slurred.

I followed Mom onto our covered porch where cigarette smoke filled the air, and about a half-dozen of her friends were seated around a table scattered with incense, candles, ashtrays, liquor bottles, and beer cans.

"Eric!" cried the boyfriend of one of Mom's closest friends from college, landing me a high-five. "How are ya, buddy?"

"I'm well—how are you?" I replied over the music, politely, just like I'd been taught.

I don't think he heard my reply, because he was half in the bag. The other guests looked lit, too. I could see the candlelight flickering over their glossy eyes, as the loud music echoed from the porch and off the retaining wall I'd recently built with my stepfather, Jim, who was thirty-eight, balding, tall, and in good shape.

"Eric! Listen, they're playing your song. Sing it with us," Jim shouted cheerfully, with a loud clap and bow of his head. "You Can't Always Get What You Want" was playing loud enough that the entire neighborhood could surely hear.

Following Jim's lead, Mom and her guests started singing, *"You can't always get what you want . . ."*

I mumbled along, cracked a fake smile, and stood there awkwardly, waiting to be dismissed.

Mom looked peaceful in the dim candlelight, with her eyes half-closed and her fingers drumming to the beat of the song, and as she opened her eyes, her smile widened, as she said, "Don't forget to brush your teeth, Eric!"

Mom's friends often said she was pretty. She was tall and

thin, with long brown hair, fair skin, high cheekbones, and brown eyes. I'd say she mostly dressed casual, and she usually frowned around me, but now on account of the booze and company, she had on the prettiest thing she could wear—a smile —one I only saw during her weekend parties, accompanied by a bottleneck beer in her left hand and a Parliament cigarette in her right hand. It was a smile that seemed to hide pain, or maybe it was guilt. Either way, when I was five, and as soon as Dad had been granted joint custody, Mom had moved us four hours away from him, from Rochester, New York, to the rural town of Queensbury, New York, which was a big change, but if there was one thing my life had encountered most, it was change.

Back in my bedroom, I felt high from the party. It only took loud music and the sight of fast cars and women in *Miami Vice* to do the trick. And with a pen dangling from my lips like a cigarette, I broke into my Keith Richards routine: kicking one leg into the air and jumping off my bed in one triumphant move-ment, strumming my air guitar to "You Can't Always Get What You Want," which I could still hear playing downstairs.

I felt like a rockstar. Stones music was my life's soundtrack. The louder it was, the larger the surge of hope that would run through me. One that imaginarily transformed me into Rocky, Rambo, the Karate Kid, or any underdog who'd managed to defeat the odds, while a little voice in my head repeated, *"I will get what I want!"*

2

EMBARRASSMENT

I t was Monday, and I could see the sagginess around Jim's and Mom's eyes. They were usually very irritable the first few days of the week, so my default protocol was to walk on eggshells, to the best of my ability.

"Why can't I get the cleats?" I asked Mom, who was sitting across from me at our dimly lit dinner table with our plates of Spam, canned green beans, and boil-in-bag white rice.

"Don't make me repeat myself. I already told you, they're too expensive. Soccer won't get you into college anyway," Mom replied, looking to Jim for support.

"But final cuts are next week, and all of the other kids have them. Why can't we use my child support money? They only cost $29.95," I said, treading lightly.

"Jim, can you please do something with him?" Mom pleaded.

Jim slipped out of his daze and slammed his heavy fist on the table, making all our silverware jump and my milk spill. "Don't talk back to your mother!" he yelled.

I flinched, always amazed how fast he could turn on me.

Only Franny, our Brittany spaniel, who was patiently waiting beneath my chair for scraps, knew the truth of our domestic life.

"I can't wait to move out of this house," I murmured, wiping milk from my shirt.

"Huh!" Mom grunted. "You'll never make it on your own. You can't even make honor roll."

Mom paused, as she stabbed some green beans with her fork, before adding: "You embarrass me. Why can't you be like Jared Gibbs?"

"*You* embarrass *me*! Why can't you be like the other moms—" I snapped back.

Without notice, Jim immediately delivered a heavy-handed slap to my head, and my left ear started to ring.

"How many times do I have to tell you? Don't talk back to your mother," he said.

"Get away from me!" I shouted.

Jim instantly kicked his chair out from under him and stood up, as I raised my arms into defense mode. All six-feet-five inches and 220 pounds of him were looming over me. He lunged, grabbed me by the hair and arm, and dragged me across the tile floor toward the kitchen sink. I used my free arm to take swings at him when I wasn't protecting my head from hitting the overhanging island countertop. Mom followed closely behind, quickly reaching for the liquid dish soap. As Jim flipped me onto my back, he pinned both my wrists to the floor and pressed one knee on top of my waist while I struggled to break free, kicking air, unable to get a clean shot at him. In addition, I was shaking my head as fast as I could to prevent Mom from getting a hold of it. But, within seconds, she had my head cradled between her knees while squeezing my nose shut with her fingers. Her knees felt like a vise. She knew I'd have to eventually open my mouth for air, and once I did—she shoved the Dawn bottle nozzle past my teeth and squirted the green liquid down my throat.

The chemicals tasted bitter, and when I tried to spit them out, Mom removed her hand from my nose and squeezed my cheeks together—keeping my jaw open for the steady stream as she kept shooting the soap down my throat. I continued struggling to break free, and eventually Jim's grip loosened and I knocked the bottle out of Mom's hand. I then quickly twisted myself out from under them, and bolted past our full dinner plates, toward the garage door.

"Let him go!" Jim yelled.

Jim wouldn't bother to chase me, knowing the neighbors would see. Plus, he knew that I'd come back for food, because I always did.

I grabbed my clearance rack sneakers off our utility room floor, and ran with one in each hand, out the garage, down the driveway, into the street, fading away into the darkening, upscale, residential neighborhood. A place we could afford to live, because Jim had built our house with his own two hands, while Mom held the checkbook for materials and the invisible whip for motivation.

Mom made sure things were done her way. I think she worried if things didn't go her way, things would go wrong. The problem was, she rarely compromised. She'd just say, "It's my way or the highway," and no matter how hard I tried, there was no way to challenge her. She didn't give options either, and if I didn't accept what was presented—I'd suffer. And there was no way around suffering; I had to go straight through it—in silence. Not by choice, but by force.

After catching my breath, I leaned against a neighbor's mailbox, slipped both sneakers on, and slowly walked along the shoulder of the curvy road. I wished I was strong enough to lay Jim out, but he was in his late thirties and fast.

All I wanted was a pair of soccer cleats, so I could be part of a team that year. The week prior, during tryouts, a star player finally passed me the ball in sight of the goal, and just when I made contact with it, I lost traction and slipped onto my imitation Umbro shorts. It was embarrassing. Actually, my entire life was. Mostly because I was grounded ninety percent of my youth for getting below an eighty in any one class, or for "talking back" —which was the hardest rule to adhere to, because the definition of backtalk shifted based on the level of sensitivity within our household at any given time. So that was the rule that led to abuse, and if I fought back too hard, the punishment would get worse with either hidden bruises or a bloody nose from a flailing hand. And Mom said if I told anyone, Child Protective Services would take me away. I had no idea what that meant, but Mom promised it'd be worse than her house, which I imagined to be scary.

As I came upon my neighbors' dark, vacant home, I scurried into their bushes and used their garden hose to rinse the remnants of dish soap out of my mouth. Crickets chirped happily around me. It was a soothing symphony, but the cool September air had me shivering. I wished I had grabbed a sweatshirt to pull over my T-shirt and skinny arms. More than that, I wished I had money to buy dinner. This was my biggest problem . . . I never had enough money to completely escape. Mom provided the basics: food, shelter, clothing, notebooks, pencils, and a Rolling Stones T-shirt that she'd once brought home from a concert, which I loved, and was careful not to damage. I suppose you could say I looked well-kept, because Mom knew I was a reflection of her. She knew because she said she was smart due to having her master's in psychology. She did admit to making some mistakes . . . she once told me she had accidentally conceived me when she was twenty-two, and then decided it was best to marry my father, immediately after, to make everything appear genuine. But that marriage only lasted a year, and Mom met Jim in a bar shortly after.

When I stepped out of the bushes, I could see into the lit-up kitchen of the Gibbs' house. Mr. Gibbs often paid me ten dollars to mow their lawn, of which Mom kept half of for my college fund and raided my room for the other half when I misbehaved.

The Gibbs' house looked warm inside. It wasn't just the amber glow radiating out of their windows; it was also the calmness in their faces as they seemed to have just finished a peaceful dinner and were now all piling onto their couch to relax, which was something I hadn't experienced, because at our house, the couch was off-limits. Mom didn't want the cushions to wear out; she said they were for company only. Even Jim knew the rules, but occasionally he'd sneak in a football game on a Sunday afternoon while Mom was out shopping. Outside of that, we only sat on the couch once a year, to smile for the family Christmas card. But when the camera went back into its velcro pouch, our reality lived on, which was frustrating, because I always felt like we were going broke just to maintain an image for people we didn't know.

I hated having to maintain our image. It didn't line up. The truth was, we lived in a neighborhood that we really couldn't afford. Jim made money at his nine-to-five, working as an engineer for a multinational conglomerate, and Mom was a "homemaker" who managed his paychecks so all our bills were paid on time. She was good at it too. She literally knew how much change he had in the cup holder of his car at any given time, and I made sure when I vacuumed his car, not to suck any up, otherwise I'd be accused of stealing—stealing from their marriage—a marriage that seemed to operate like a workshop, where Jim worked and Mom shopped.

As the temperature continued to drop, I tucked my face inside my T-shirt and blew warm air against my chest. When I raised my head, I looked back at the Gibbs' and a feeling of loneliness ran through me. I wanted to be part of a loving family. A family where I didn't have to live in fear. A family where I felt safe, but that was a distant dream. In the immediate moment, I needed to find food and a safe place to sleep.

My brain started spinning. Part of me wondered if I should sneak into the Gibbs' shed to sleep, but the other part wanted to ring their doorbell and ask to use their phone to call my father, who was a counselor at a Juvenile Detention Center. The problem was, there was a chance he'd call the cops, and then the cops would call Child Protective Services. Plus, Jim raised me to never complain, so that option was looking grim.

I wasn't emotionally close to Jim, but he often shared bullet points of knowledge and wisdom with me. Just the week before, while I was tilling the garden with him, he said, "Eric, the world doesn't owe you anything. It'll spin with or without you. You can be a victim or a leader; the choice is yours."

I think this is when I started realizing I wanted to be a leader. I wanted to create something from scratch. Most importantly, I wanted to create a new life for myself, but for the time being—I had to cope with this one.

AFTER MOST OF the lights had gone out in our neighborhood, I knew I had a choice to make, and since I didn't have many options . . . I chose to walk home.

On my walk, I began wondering what it'd be like to live with my father. Mom said he was a "bad man," so whenever I was required to visit a court-mandated therapist, I just said what she instructed me to, that I wanted to live with her. Therefore I didn't know much about him, because the visitation rights prevented me from seeing him much.

I hated feeling trapped, and I hated having to kneel upright on the hard surface of the tile floor, in the corner, for hours on end when I upset Mom. And I'm too embarrassed to describe the time she made me stay in the tiny bathroom of Grandma's RV—with the door shut—for the entire drive from New York to Florida. Mom's discipline practices were humiliating, to say the least, but she always said, "It's for your own good." However, I was never convinced. I considered myself Mom's possession and deduced she was hell-bent on showing her friends, neighbors, and the entire world that she'd make me a success at any cost. A cost that seemed to depend on pain, fear, and arguments. Arguments that consisted of yelling, rather than communication.

When I arrived back home, there was only one light on in the house. The one illuminating my cold plate of Spam, in the same exact spot I had left it on the kitchen table. And as I quietly ate the Spam in silence, I could hear some soft talking between Mom and Jim emitting from behind their closed bedroom door. I assumed they must have just tucked in, and soon, I also found myself in my bedroom, lying on my back in bed, wide awake, with my eardrum still ringing from Jim's smack. My mind wouldn't stop churning. I couldn't understand how Mom, who hadn't accomplished much herself, could tell me how to do everything in life. And as I closed my eyes, I could feel my anger and determination blending into one as I prayed: *I will make enough money to get out of this house, I will live life on my terms, and I will sail away with the woman of my dreams.* And those were the words that became my nightly mantra. My bedtime prayer.

3

INSTINCTS

Grandma, on Mom's side, was a sweet Polish widow and a little spacey. I still can't figure out how she managed to use a half-a-can of Aqua Net hairspray every morning while smoking a cigarette—without blowing herself up. Thankfully she didn't, because whenever she had visited us, she'd bring me candy. Although, instead of eating it, I'd secretly bring it to school and sell it to my classmates . . . at least until Mom eventually found out and asked, "Do you want to grow up to be a drug dealer?"

I was only in sixth grade when Mom had popped that question, so I didn't completely understand what she meant. I only knew I had to stop selling the candy, which was frustrating, because every time I conformed, I felt like I stopped growing into the person I was born to be: someone who knew how to trust their own instincts.

ONCE I HIT NINTH GRADE, I discreetly decided to start selling candy again. Except this time I snuck money out of my piggy bank, and bought the candy at a gas station I passed every day on my walk to school.

My plan was simple: buy the candy, resell it to my classmates at a profit, and then replace the money I took for the candy purchases before Mom knew it was missing. All my profits would be hidden in a separate spot that she wouldn't find—the bottom of my Monopoly board game box—a game that I grew up playing alone on my bedroom floor for hours on end, rolling the dice for each of the imaginary players, until I owned the entire board and my opponents were either bankrupt or out of Get Out of Jail Free cards.

Of course, all my wins were false, but they were the closest feeling I ever had to a real win, and my life was based on feelings. To be more exact, mixed feelings, but that's because I craved connection and didn't know what connection was.

Initially, I only targeted a few popular kids for my candy sales, because they always had extra cash on top of their lunch money. And since they had a lot of friends, word spread quickly that I was dealing, and students I'd never met before started seeking me out to get their fix. Luckily, I was tall, six-foot-five, and lanky, so they could easily find my head above the crowded hallways, in between classes.

I always carried an open pack of Pez as samples for the pretty girls, and I didn't make them pay, because I liked their attention. Plus, they were good for marketing; their followers always took notice of what made them smile, and if they were eating my Pez, that meant more sales for me. Although it didn't take long for one of the teachers, who was a customer of mine, to tip me off that faculty was aware of my operation and determining how to shut it down. So I decided to sell even more discreetly: only first thing in the morning, out of my locker. That way all the evidence would be gone before the day started, and only wrappers and allegations would remain.

.   .   .

ONE MORNING, a small group of kids were at my locker and huddled around my open backpack to see what I had on offer, and suddenly, I heard from behind me, "Yo, Lips!" accompanied by a firm slap on my shoulder.

I flinched by default, because a raised hand near me was usually a threat. But when I turned, it was Pete Lansing, senior, star athlete, beautiful girlfriend—with a big smile, all amped up.

"Lips!" Pete said again.

"What's up?" I replied, not understanding.

"You're Lips," he said, pointing to the Rolling Stones logo on the front of my T-shirt. "I need four packs of Pez, Lips."

I'm not sure if Pete knew what the logo stood for, or my real name, but it was an honor to be recognized and have a decent nickname bestowed upon me by one of the popular kids in school. I felt noticed. Actually, it was the first time I felt like I mattered in the world.

After Pete had acknowledged me, it didn't take long for the rest of his crew to notice me as well. Especially, when I could afford to buy two lunches, because only the rich kids stood in line for a second tray. On top of that, I was invited to sit at the popular kids table in the cafeteria. I chose to stay at the quiet kids table, though, because I felt more at home there. I would've felt uncomfortable being surrounded by a dozen trendsetters with brand-name clothing, spin the bottle stories, and freedom to pursue whatever they wanted in life. I was still sitting in a good spot, though, because my self-esteem got a boost every time a popular kid walked over to our table and slapped me a high-five. And when girls noticed that interaction, it didn't take long for all of them to acknowledge me as "Lips." Except Mom. She still called me "troubled," and surprised me one afternoon as I walked in the door from school.

"What's this?" Mom asked, holding up a crumpled receipt,

from a twenty-dollar purchase of candy from Stewart's gas station.

I instantly knew she had searched my bedroom and stumbled upon the receipt in my garbage can under my desk. I always hated how she searched my garbage can.

"Where is it?" she demanded, raising her voice. "Where's the candy?"

"I don't have any," I replied, trapped between her and the closed door behind me.

She shook her head, and said louder, "I told you, you're not allowed to sell anything at school! Empty your pockets! Now!"

I reached into both of my pockets and turned them inside out, showing her I didn't have any money.

"Take off your backpack," she said, motioning to search it. "Don't make me say it again!"

I spun off my backpack and watched Mom unzip each compartment, flip through each book, and finally open the smallest compartment to the sight of over twenty dollars in singles.

I was fuming. Mom had just shut down my entire business in a matter of seconds. Why? Because I had all my eggs in one compartment . . . the compartment she seized. And this was the day I learned I could make money but that diversification would be the only way to preserve it.

4

ACCEPTANCE

I learned how to navigate the forest at a young age, because aside from pottery and Sunday church, camping was Mom's main hobby. She regularly guided the family to various remote canoe-access-only destinations throughout the Adirondacks, where we'd spend time eating charred hot dogs at weathered picnic tables and she'd say: "Eric, real freedom is in the woods, not in civilization."

Camping was Jim's therapy, too, although before meeting Mom, his main hobbies included riding his Harley on the weekends and driving his RX-7 on the weekdays. But he sold those toys when he met Mom in order to become a family man.

I felt safe in the woods around Jim, because there were no corners for him to trap me in when he'd have a flare-up. I could easily outrun him and hide behind a boulder or a downed tree until he cooled down, all the while watching him from a distance working with ropes, knives, fire, water, and unexpected weather conditions.

I learned a lot from watching Jim. It's fair to say he taught me most of what I know about surviving in the woods. Rule number one: set up camp before you start drinking.

I furthered my survival skills down the road from our house, where there were several hundred acres of vacant forest with miles of overgrown trails winding through it. I explored those trails with lone wolf Kyle whenever I was allowed out. Kyle was shorter than me, but stocky and fast. I liked him because he never asked why I was grounded for weeks at a time, and when I did happen to get ungrounded, I could just run two blocks over and ring his doorbell.

Kyle always brought his .22-caliber on our excursions. We used it to shoot cans, and when it was his turn, he riddled them with holes while I focused on my new plan—to find my own secluded piece of land within the forest, where I could build a fort to spend the night in case of an emergency. And by tenth grade, I had found that spot—a place no one would find—between three large pines. And whenever I could get away, I'd sneak Jim's tools from our garage in order to chop down various-size trees to build a tree fort about ten feet above the ground, which consisted of a frame, deck, railing, and a sturdy ladder.

Kyle and I would spend hours at the fort, and anytime I cleaned up after one of Mom's ragers, I'd swipe a few beers and bring them there to drink at a later date. I stashed them in a large Rubbermaid container that we buried in the ground, covering it with moss and pine needles. I stashed other supplies there too—a boombox, flashlight, batteries, candles, rope, snacks, bottled water, and a *Playboy* magazine. Everything I might need in an emergency was stored in the ground, and whenever I was in good standing with Mom, I'd tell her that I was sleeping over at Kyle's, but instead we'd head to the fort and camp out among crowds of trees.

.   .   .

"WE SHOULD RIDE the trails to Deadman's Drop in the morning," Kyle said one night at the fort, cracking a beer while sitting next to the campfire.

"What's that?" I asked, finishing my fifth beer, with the boombox laying across my lap, playing some Neil Young.

"It's a dam near Butler Pond, about two miles up the mountain . . . that way," he pointed. "Some guy jumped and killed himself there. That's why it's called Deadman's Drop. It's a 170-foot vertical drop."

"Damn!" I replied. "I want to see it!"

"Fuck, I can't imagine wanting to die. I still haven't been laid," Kyle laughed.

I laughed back, but the truth was, I had contemplated suicide. To me it said, "I quit—do you love me now?" But I played it cool, because Kyle had touched another nerve—sex—something I knew nothing about, except for what I'd seen in a few Hollywood movies. The problem was, the sheets were always covering the act, so sex was still a foreign topic to me.

As the conversation stalled, I stood up, reached for another beer, and chugged the entire can, while thinking of something to say. Out of ideas, I stepped twenty feet back from the fire and ran toward it as fast as I could and jumped, landing on the other side in a roll.

"Shit, Lips! You should run hurdles," Kyle said, looking blurry through the tall flames. "You'd win."

Again, I didn't know how to reply. I wasn't familiar with compliments. I was more attuned to Mom's constant question of, "Why can't you be like the other kids?"

I hated that question. It actually got me to believe I wasn't good at anything, even when I'd receive a compliment. And I think that internal conflict was the recipe for most of my discomforts in life. I had a solution now, though—more booze—

the one thing that could temporarily shed my insecurities so I could live in the moment.

A FEW MINUTES LATER, I heard some laughing in the distance. I then saw the beam from a flashlight, and looked toward Kyle.

"Oh yeah, I forgot to tell you—I invited Kim and Liz," Kyle mumbled, swaying side to side.

Kim and Liz were a couple girls from high school who lived in the neighboring subdivision. I barely knew them, but they were always cool with me when they brushed by me on the school bus.

"Wow! This place is surreal," Liz said, stopping short, as they arrived with cigarettes and a bottle of Jack in hand. "It took us forever to find you guys."

After we greeted them, I slipped into the pitch-black woods to pull a few more beers out of our underground container. When I returned, I stoked the fire, turned up the Jim Morrison playing through the boombox, and rolled a large log toward the fire to sit on. Kyle was sitting on the ground across from me, and Liz and Kim were sitting between us in some lawn chairs Kyle had brought. Before I could get one word in, Liz passed me her bottle and I took a swig from it. I then passed it back to her, and she passed it around another four-plus times. I took a swig on each pass.

"Want some, Lips?" Liz asked. I was now seeing double, but I knew she was holding out a spliff. I felt nervous because I'd never tried weed, and if Mom found out I did, the little freedom I had would've been out the window.

"Nah, I'm good. Thank you, though," I replied, gripping my beer.

I could tell Liz was eyeing me, but I didn't know how to

proceed. Plus, she wasn't really my type. She wore ponchos and flared jeans, and her hair was always a tad disheveled.

A HALF-HOUR LATER, we were all standing around the crackling fire, chitchatting and swaying to the music. Kyle and the girls seemed fine. They were taking a few sidesteps from the booze, but no one looked like the scary stories I'd heard about drug use in health class. So the next time the joint passed me, I took a small drag, and since I didn't feel anything, when it circled back, I hit it again. And by my fifth drag, I looked toward Kyle and saw his face stretched into a funny grin.

"Right onnnnnnn," I said, clutching my stomach, crumpling to the ground from the force of my own laughter. I think the combination of seeing two of his faces and the weed did the trick.

The ground felt cold, but within seconds the bass line of the Doors' "Roadhouse Blues," thumping from the boombox, struck a chord within me, and in one swift motion, I shot up from the ground, shouting the song's lyrics: "Keep your eyes on the road and hands uponnn the wheel!"

I did a rapid double spin toward the boombox, twisted the volume knob to *max,* and started dancing just like I'd done alone in my room for years. But this time, on account of the weed, the song came alive like I'd never heard it before, and I felt unstoppable. I didn't care if the girls were laughing at me or with me. Electricity was running through every vein of my body as I began swinging from a pine tree branch with one hand, with an imaginary mic in my other hand, still singing. They all started singing and dancing, too, and as the song came to an end, I collapsed to the ground and rolled onto my back. That's when I saw three heads above me echoing, "Lips, Lips, Lips . . . are you all right?"

"Yeah," I moaned, completely at peace, watching embers float up into the dark sky.

I paid the price the following morning with a monumental headache, but at that point in my life, I would've done anything to fit in. Even if it meant changing myself to fit into places I didn't necessarily belong. To me, fitting in was about trying to adapt to a world I knew nothing about. Hell, I'd been trying to fit in since the playground, hoping the dominant group would accept me. I had a simple strategy, too—mimic them. Walk like them, talk like them, and dress like them. I was starting to get good at it, too. I had different versions of myself I could present, depending on the group I was around. I think this is why Mom always said, "Dress for the occasion."

5

SURVIVAL

Throughout the next year, Kyle started inviting more people to the fort, and I continued using weed and booze to get the parties started. Drugs helped me ease the anxieties that came from socializing with unfamiliar people. They also helped me gain some popularity, mainly from my hearty laugh, which was usually funnier than my joke. It was a contagious laugh that helped me develop a small crew of friends who'd swing by my house on Friday nights to see if I could hang.

Mom was always suspicious of my newfound friends, and usually asked for their names so she could check if they were on the honor roll. But if she was drinking with company and my grades were up to par, I'd have permission to take off.

Someone always had a license and a car, zipping us through a circuit, picking up as many people as they could fit, along with a twelve-pack for each of us. I always gave one of the kids with a chalked fake ID six bucks for my Milwaukee's Best, and slipped another five to whoever was packing the five-foot bong. The bong would smoke like a chimney into the night as we funneled beers around it and bodies fell to the ground. It was a spectacle, and all the money I'd received from mowing lawns or shoveling driveways went straight to my brain in the form of liquid and smoke. And while my buddies hooked up with the girls they invited, I blacked out alone, because I couldn't shake my fear of doing it wrong and being talked about. That would've been the quickest way to lose friends. So when my buddies spoke of their newest girl, I would just reply that I was too drunk and out of luck.

IT WAS a sunny Friday when I found myself stretching with the track team. What Kyle had said to me about hurdles got me thinking . . . track was the one sport in school I didn't need money to participate in. I could just use my everyday sneakers. All the other sports required purchasing special equipment. But not track, and Mom allowed it because, last she knew, all my grades were above 80.

Coach led us through the warmup: pushups, situps, then a speech about proper technique. I focused on every word he said, just like Jim had taught me when sneaking in some Sunday football while Mom was out shopping. I can still hear Jim's voice from when he was standing in front of the TV—with the remote in his hand—ready to turn it off at a moment's notice when Mom pulled up into the driveway. "Eric, focus on goals, not obstacles."

Yeah, Jim secretly knew Mom's rules were extreme, but he'd never say that, because unlike me, he knew some things were better off unsaid. Actually, he was a master of unsaid words. I, on the other hand, was a slave to the ones I let slip out.

I stuck out on the track field with my scrawny long legs, and placed poorly in races the first month. I think my fear of looking stupid was holding me back, but it was inspiring to be surrounded by others who all had the same goal: to win. And with time, I adapted to my new environment and decided to stay away from weed and booze. Instead, I laser-focused on track practice and spent my alone time visualizing myself clearing hurdle after hurdle, not just for a win, but also for an award.

THE NEXT FRIDAY, I was ready to push the envelope, because if I screwed up, I assumed my team would forget by the next time I'd see them on Monday. So with some teammates watching, I took my position at the starting line, and when the whistle blew, I accelerated like I was on fire. My rhythm was tight. "Lead with the knee, weight forward, trail leg knee high," I repeated to myself, sinking into the moment. I only had to think about one thing—the finish line. There was no past or future. Being an athlete was about living in the present, with focus. And when I crossed the line I looked over my shoulder and saw the star hurdler on the team behind me. I'd beaten him and everyone else, and the feeling was better than drugs.

When I came to a complete stop, I took a couple gasps and heard Coach yell from the bleachers, "Nice work, Canori!"

"Thank you, Coach," I replied, secretly wanting to scream out, "Fuck yeah!"

With a smile, I stretched my T-shirt up from my chest, wiping the sweat off my forehead. I then heard, "Hey, Lips!" and I turned around.

There she was, Jamie, casually walking by with the girls' track team. The sunlight was radiating a halo around her, but I could still see her shiny thick black ponytail, her short running shorts, and her beautiful smile. "Lookin' good," she added, with a wink.

"Thank you," I replied quietly, squinting into the sun behind her.

I couldn't believe Jamie had noticed me. All it took was one win.

I kept my head down as I walked toward Coach, who wanted us in a huddle. I tried to listen to him as he critiqued a teammate's performance, but I just kept hearing Jamie's voice echoing in my head. But then I heard another voice, which pulled me out of my fantasy world.

"Eric!"

I looked around, but I couldn't see where it was coming from.

"Eric!" I heard again. Some others heard it, too.

I held my hand up as a visor and began scanning the perimeter of the field, and there was Jim, leaning against the chain-link fence with his hands gripping it. An alarm immediately went off inside my head and I backed away from the huddle.

As I jogged toward Jim, I hoped not too many people were staring. For a second, I wondered if he had seen my win and wanted to congratulate me, but the thought vanished as I got closer. I could see that his eyes were bulging.

I stopped a couple feet away from the fence, standing warily. "What are you doing here?" I asked quietly.

"Get your stuff and get in the car. Now!" he said.

"What are you talking about? We're not done with practice."

"I don't care. You're done."

I turned to look back at the athletes on the field. They were focused on Coach, but still within earshot. I couldn't risk a scene, so I discreetly grabbed my stuff from the bleachers and slipped out the gate.

I shut the car door, and sat silently as we pulled away.

"Do you have anything to say?" Jim asked.

"No," I replied, now knowing why he was there. My report card must have arrived in the mail earlier that day, and I knew I had gotten a 68 in Social Studies and a 72 in English.

I clutched my backpack and watched Jim flick the ashes of

his Camel out the crack of the window. He was just the bounty hunter; the stepdad. He was dispatched to get me, and now that he'd completed his job, all I could do was watch his cigarette smoke drift out the window, wishing I could go with it.

I knew track was done for the season, but I wasn't focused on that. I needed to prepare for what awaited me at home, which meant I needed a change of clothes in case I had to escape the house quickly. I hoped things wouldn't escalate, but now that I was seventeen, I was too strong to be a pushover.

When we pulled up to the house I shot inside in stealth mode, ahead of Jim, bypassing Mom, who was making a "To-Do" list in the kitchen.

Once I was in my room, everything slowed down. I became extra focused, knowing that every move and every second mattered. I changed into jeans and a flannel, then scanned my room. I threw my Walkman, a few cassette tapes, a fleece jacket, and some underwear in my backpack. I then heard, "Eric! Get down here!"

I quickly zipped my backpack closed, threw it over my shoulders, and headed down into the kitchen—to see Mom standing —holding up my report card like a search warrant.

"Track's done, I'm selling your bike, and your speakers are mine. Plan on being in your room for the rest of the year. We took your window crank, too, so don't try to force the window open," she said with flat words and a tight face. "I want you home every day at 2 p.m. sharp! Do you understand?"

Her entire body was shaking with anger. I could almost feel her grinding teeth. She waited for a response, but I remained silent, with my backpack cinched on, staring at her without a flinch.

I didn't care about all the things she had seized, but I couldn't accept being taken off the track team and losing my chance with Jamie.

"You're done! Do you hear me?!" Mom yelled, slapping the report card down against the counter.

"*You're* done!" I shouted back, unable to restrain myself.

Without warning, Mom whipped her backhand around to my face and I felt the sting of her wedding ring scrape my cheekbone.

This was my biggest flaw, not knowing when to keep my mouth shut. Regardless, I quickly reached for her arm, trapped it, and as expected, she yelled, and right on cue, I heard Jim, coming in from the garage.

Jim charged toward me fast, but I shoved him, and quickly ran past him and into the garage.

With my adrenaline pumping, I jumped on my mountain bike and pedaled to the fort as fast as I could. It felt like every blood vessel in my body was constricting as I raced down the rutted trail and made it to the fort in record time. And in celebration of my retreat to higher ground, I tilted my head back and screamed at the top of my lungs into the canopy, "Welcome home, Eric!"

I could see birds fluttering among the trees. They knew I was there, but no one knew I'd just successfully fled the scene, with one goal—safety. I was only fooling myself, though, because I wouldn't be able to survive there for long. I was still attached to Mom by the umbilical cord, and deep down, I was just a confused kid afraid I wouldn't make it. It was the type of fear that would drain almost anyone of all hopeful solutions. It was my fear of the unknown, my greatest fear of all, and the fear that controlled me.

After I pulled my matches, weed, and pipe out from my underground crate, I lit a fire and slowly started feeding kindling into the growing flame. The flame calmed me, and when the fire was steady, I climbed up into the fort and leaned against the railing. I could hear the birds and squirrels in the

vicinity, and I knew it was time to get high. So I slowly packed a
bowl, lit it, and took a long pull. I held the smoke deep in my
lungs for as long as I could, and when I exhaled, I thought about
running down the track and how good it felt to win. Not just for
me, but for Jamie.

As the temperature dropped, I reached for the fleece jacket
in my backpack and pulled it over my flannel. I put my Mazzy
Star cassette in my Walkman and rewound it to the first song,
"Fade into You." I listened to the lyrics closely, staring at the fire
below. I started mumbling along, *"Fade into you . . . a stranger's
heart without a home . . . ,"* and toward the end of the song,
sadness and loneliness pressed down on me. I wanted Jamie
there with me.

Even though I didn't know what love was, I craved female
touch. I was tired of being alone, and I was tired of thinking life
was supposed to be a struggle every single day. I was even more
tired of the social isolation that I knew was coming, because
now that I'd had a small taste of freedom and friendship, I
couldn't give it up. I wasn't going back to spending days, weeks,
and years alone in my room gazing inward at my thoughts of
what life should or could be. No, I hated being boxed in without
money or a girlfriend, and now track and socializing was done
until the next report card, assuming it was good enough. Fuck, I
couldn't fathom the idea of going back to school and telling my
friends I'd be grounded for the next three months, because I
cared what people thought about me, and this was an extreme
embarrassment. There was no point in life anymore. I wanted to
end it.

Suicide wasn't just some erratic thought of mine; I'd considered it in the past during my long stretches of being grounded.
But there was always something too flashy about hanging myself
outside my bedroom window. I didn't want Jim to find me and
call me a "quitter." I preferred the idea of "missing," without

being on the missing persons list. Just an unexplained disappearance, with few questions asked.

I CONTEMPLATED death for the next two nights at the fort, while finding things to keep myself busy. I raked the pine needles surrounding the fort with a tree branch. I collected firewood deep in the forest. I reorganized the rocks around the firepit, and ate all the snacks in my buried crate. And as I started losing track of time under the stars, I determined dying was the best solution, and that Deadman's Drop would be the easiest way.

I was done living under Mom's extreme rules. I was done with everything. There was no more room to grow. It was time to disappear—permanently. I will admit, though, deep down, I wanted to be found. I wanted to be recognized and accepted for who I was. I wanted to enjoy life. Fuck, I wasn't going back to Mom's house to rot away in a bedroom. There was nothing there for me, except food. And I wasn't about to let my hunger steer me back into a home I didn't belong in. That would've been the most painful way to die, and the way I wasn't going to. My life would end my way, on my terms.

When I started riding my bike to Deadman's Drop, I quickly remembered the route Kyle showed me, and when I got there, I laid my bike down and walked toward the dam, sticks cracking under my feet. The drop was part of our town water supply, which was a remote pristine lake surrounded by pine trees, mossy rocks, and silence. On shore was the concrete spillway that led to the 170-foot vertical drop. As I stood at the edge of the spillway, I leaned over the rusty iron railing, looking down into what seemed like a small concrete room without a floor. I tried adjusting my eyes to see into the darkness, but it was just a black hole that descended deep into the earth. It felt cold.

I stepped back, reached for a rock, and then dropped it into the hole, counting to six before I heard it ricochet off the concrete. "This should work," I said to myself, with some hesitation, wondering if it'd be a clean kill.

I gripped the railing again, this time tighter, as I lifted one leg over and then the other. I then carefully twisted myself around, holding the railing behind my back, leaning out over the edge, as far as my arms allowed. My stomach flipped and my throat swelled. I was scared. I couldn't believe I was about to do this, but I was, as I shut my eyes with my torso dangling over the blackness. This is it, I thought. No more pain, no more fear, and sadly, no more dreams.

Fuck, all I wanted was a different home, my own refrigerator, and to play sports. I couldn't even go on a date or invite a girl to the house. What was I supposed to do? Live with the humiliation of Jamie and the rest of the track team running by my house in the upcoming weeks—seeing me installing the inground sprinkler system for Jim—with a pickaxe, in my imitation Umbro shorts and vinyl sneakers? Are you kidding . . . and then Jim will tell me day after day that the trenches aren't deep enough and all the boulders need to be moved offsite? Fuck, how green did our lawn need to be for the neighbors' approval? Mom had always said I was going to grow up to be a "ditch digger," but what she'd failed to realize was that she was teaching me to be one. My life consisted of schoolwork and slave labor, while Mom bought things she didn't need, with money she didn't have, to impress people she didn't even know. I was done with the merry-go-round.

I paused my thoughts, took a breath, and my body loosened. Sadness and frustration flooded me all at once. I held the railing tighter as tears and spit poured from my face, dropping into the emptiness below. After a few seconds, I burst out, "Fuck you, Mom!" I screamed it as loud as I could, with the echo pinging back to me from the surrounding mountains. "Fuck you!" I screamed again. "I fucking hate you!" My throat soon gave out, and right then a fire started burning inside me. I didn't want to jump. I wasn't ready to die. I was just done wasting my life living Mom's life.

I carefully turned myself back around to face the railing, stepped back over it, and wiped my face on my shirt sleeve. As I stood on the pine needles quietly, I felt a deep determination brewing inside me, which I hadn't experienced before. It was signaling me to rise up. It was telling me to cut the umbilical cord. It was telling me it was time to survive on my own—in any way possible. Not just survive, but thrive. To do whatever I had to do, to get whatever I wanted and needed in life.

I kicked around some pine cones, acknowledging I'd become a product of an environment I didn't choose. And once again, I felt money was the solution to all my problems. And the only way I knew how to make money was to solve other people's problems at a profit. That's when I started thinking about all the kids in school who often asked me to score them weed. They knew I could get it for them, because they saw me higher than a giraffe's ass day in and day out. And they were correct; I could've asked Liz's older brother for a bag, no problem. But I'd always declined helping them, out of fear of Mom finding out.

My conscience began to weigh in. "You're already buying it; that's illegal," I first heard. "What's the difference between buying and selling? They're both crimes. Plus, weed isn't bad for you. Hell, smoking pot was the first time you ever felt good in your life." "So what if you get arrested? Jail beats death," I heard the final voice say. And that was it, case settled. I was going to sell weed, make money, and learn how to survive on my own. I wouldn't call myself a drug dealer. I'd call myself a florist, because weed is just a flower. This wasn't an illusion; it was a vision. A vision with a strategy that began to form as I biked back home to complete step one: patch things up with Mom. It was imperative that I resolved our conflict before I started my business. Too much tension between us would only stall my plans and leave me feeling hopeless.

AFTER CIRCLING our neighborhood several times, I eventually saw Mom outside doing yard work, so I slowly rolled up to our mailbox at the bottom of the driveway, keeping a foot on one pedal, ready to flee if necessary.

"I don't think Jim wants you back here," she said, approaching me. She was neither angry nor happy—just permanently dissatisfied.

"I'm sorry for the way I behaved. I can be better. I won't act like that again," I replied, knowing the fastest way for me to succeed was to look like I was going to play by her rules, while silently playing by my own.

She nodded and replied, "Wait here," before turning and walking up to the house to speak with Jim.

I felt like I was applying for a job interview, hoping they'd accept me. I was nervous, but I remained confident. It was critical that I did. I needed to relay the impression that I would happily follow all their rules and orders, because keeping them satisfied would provide me with food and shelter until I could build up enough capital to survive on my own.

WHEN MOM CAME BACK OUTSIDE, she signaled for me to enter. I wasn't sure if I was heading into an ambush, so I remained prepared for the unknown.

As I walked into the house, Jim was standing with his hands on his hips, staring at me silently. I tried my best to pass him confidently, but I ended up tilting my head down as I followed Mom up the stairs toward my room.

After Mom opened my bedroom door, I stood in silence. My stereo, magazines, and deck of cards were gone. All that remained was a bed, a desk, a chair, my school books, and a sixty-watt light bulb with a shade hanging from the ceiling. The only thing keeping the room softer than a jail cell was the maroon carpet and posters on the walls.

"Outside of school, you'll stay in this room unless you need to use the bathroom. Jim doesn't want to see you at dinner either, so I'll bring your food up to you. Do you understand?" Mom said, standing at the door, clutching its knob.

"I understand," I replied, accepting obediently.

I had nothing else to say; a loose tongue would have crippled my plans anyway. Plus, I already knew what was going on—they were simply exhausted—probably because they had stuffed too many expectations into their lives, trying to live out some fairy tale, not realizing it was a nightmare for me. I wished they would've loosened up. Why did we need to worry about the future so much? Overthinking it was leading to problems that didn't even exist. It was inciting fear in all of us, and that fear had officially become our worst enemy.

6

DETERMINATION

I spent the next month in my bedroom alone, looking out the window, watching the leaves blossom, while strategically plotting how to sell weed without getting caught. Eventually, I determined I only needed a few satisfied customers who didn't run their mouths, in order to stay out of the authorities' crosshairs.

My plan was to start buying bottom-of-the-barrel $90 half-ounces from Liz's older brother on my walks home from school, which I started doing. I'd then immediately jog to the fort and stash them in a coffee can—careful to never be followed—and never arrive home more than fifteen minutes later than Mom expected, because as long as I remained in my room and studied, she'd never be suspicious of my activities.

I only sold to a few low-key burners who knew to give me a day's notice for their order so I could prepare. The process was simple: I'd sneak sandwich baggies from Mom's pantry, run to the fort on my way to school, make a bag, hide it in the elastic of my sock, then transport it to the school parking lot for a quick $30 sale. The transactions were always smooth. The only problem was with my supplier, which I hoped to replace, because he was inconsistent. Plus, I didn't like buying weed out of his car in a public space—a convenience store parking lot. On top of that, after I discarded the seeds and stems from the weed he'd sold me, there was barely enough bud left for me to break even because I never passed the seeds and stems onto my customers. Instead, I tossed them out and took the loss. My top priority was to create satisfied customers, because I knew customers talked, and I wanted to give them something good to talk about. That would help me become the person I wanted to be—a businessman—a man who was resourceful, determined to succeed, and, most importantly, willing to take risks for profits.

THE SUMMER BEFORE SENIOR YEAR, Mom suggested I apply for a job at McDonald's, and I was happy to do so, just to get out of the house. My starting position was to keep the bathrooms and dining area sparkling clean, before I quickly moved up to grill man, beside my co-worker, Jake, who was a white purebred townie who never managed to acquire his GED.

Jake smoked me up on all our breaks, and I constantly asked him to introduce me to his weed connect, but he always gave the same response: "He don't like meetin' new faces, bud."

One lunch break, Jake and I went to the back of the parking lot and hopped in his beat-up '84 Chrysler minivan, which had a cracked windshield, rusted-out wheel wells, bald tires, a low-hanging muffler, and a taped-up taillight. The van almost matched Jake's stained teeth and pale skin, and when he opened the sliding door, a rush of summer heat blasted our faces as he quickly cleared some trash off the seat while saying, "Hop in . . . hurry. Boss is gonna be lookin' for us soon."

Once inside the van, Jake reached under his seat and twisted open a black film canister containing two neon green, frosty white buds. I could immediately smell the dankness.

"Holy fuck! What kind of weed is that?" I asked.

"Don't know, don't care . . . it puts you in God's Country though," he said, packing up a dirty porcelain pipe.

"Come on, when are you going to introduce me to your connect? It'll help me out," I semi-begged, trying not to kill the moment.

"No, this'll help you out," he said, passing me a Bic lighter and the freshly packed pipe.

I touched the flame to the weed, inhaled deeply, then coughed up my soul while reaching to open the window.

"No!" he shouted. "We hotboxing this . . . the doors and windows stay shut."

We took several more hits until I could barely see through the window, and when Jake finally popped open the door, smoke billowed out like an SOS.

Once I stepped outside of the smoke, the sun looked brighter than I'd ever seen it, and my sneakers looked like a size twenty. I was high and I liked it. Weed was my escape to see the world in a different way. It made me laugh, too, and I craved laughter. It was free medicine.

As we clocked back in, the lunch hour rush was in full swing and I was higher than a kite. Every few minutes, the cashier shouted back to me in the kitchen the number of burgers she needed. I'd then toast the buns and garnish them with ketchup, mustard, pickles, and onions, while flipping the patties and sometimes melting a slice of yellow rubbery "cheese" over them. After that, I'd place the patties in the buns and send them up front on a tray to the cashier, where they'd be wrapped and sold.

.   .   .

AFTER GRILLING at a fast clip for over an hour, I noticed I had twelve burgers over-cooking and no buns anywhere in sight, even though I distinctly remembered preparing twelve buns with all the toppings. I couldn't believe it, but I had to . . . my fried brain forgot to put the burgers on the condiment-covered buns before I sent them up front. Needless to say, it only took a few minutes for the customers to start returning their meatless burgers, and only a few minutes after that for the boss to say, "Eric, it's time for you to find another job to smoke at."

I was shocked to hear those words, and Jake thought it was hilarious that I was fired. So much so that he decided to quit on the spot and walk out the door with me.

As I stood distraught next to Jake's minivan, he just laughed at me in my purple uniform, and I tried my best to ignore him, because I was confused, not knowing what I was going to tell Mom.

"Relax, man, you don't always need a plan," Jake said, leaning against his van, not comprehending my conundrum.

"Oh, are you going to pay my Mom?" I asked.

"What?"

"Half of my paychecks go directly to my mom, for my college savings," I replied, knowing Mom expected her cut of the $4.25 per hour I was making.

"Shit, and I was complaining about government taxes," he replied, now understanding of my predicament. "Sounds like a racket to me, bud."

I looked down, and Jake stopped talking. I sensed he was thinking, as he turned toward his driver door to open it.

"Well, she can't collect taxes on illegal money," he said, twisting his face back toward me. "How about we get outta here and I introduce you to my dealer? You already know he has the best bud around."

I lit right up! "Yes! Please!" I replied.

This is what I'd been waiting for . . . to be plugged into a consistent source. One with fair pricing, better quality, and most importantly—reliability.

I liked Jake. He didn't waste time focusing on what we are told life should be; he just lived it. To him, life was about being in the moment. There was no past or future, and I know Mom wouldn't have agreed with his lack of aspirations, but I never judged his choices, because I never knew the options he faced. I only knew I had $150 in my wallet and three hours to kill before Mom would be picking me up from the end of my shift. Knowing that, I chose to hitch a ride with Jake for one purpose only: to meet his weed dealer in the small neighboring city of Glens Falls, in hopes of a dependable cash flow.

As we approached the dealer's house, I told Jake I didn't want to park near it. He then gave me a weird look when I started explaining that cops run license plates going in and out of known dealers' residences. I even asked if he'd ever seen *Miami Vice*, and he burst out laughing, saying the show was all fiction.

Jake parked in the dealer's driveway anyway, but I bit my tongue, knowing the risk was worth the reward.

The dealer's house was a run-down one-story that looked like it would fall over if we knocked on the door too hard. The chain-link fence was mangled, the swimming pool had collapsed and was overgrown with weeds, and a gutter hung from the roof by a single nail. Inside it smelled like cigarettes, dogs, and cooking grease. The dealer, Doug, was sitting on his couch watching *Looney Tunes* with a chubby kid in a diaper on each side of him. He looked like a Looney Tune himself. He was a pasty white guy, with greasy brown hair and more stains on his tank top than a used napkin at Chuck E. Cheese.

"Who are you?" Doug asked.

"Mike, nice to meet you," I said, reaching for his hand, giving him an alias on the spot, knowing not to give my real name.

Doug shifted his enormous heft forward and shook my hand. "How much you want?" he asked without eye contact.

"How much for an ounce?"

I could sense he was wondering if I was a rat, or a cop in training, and it took him a moment to reply, but he eventually said, "One-twenty."

I stayed cool and calm, not wanting him to notice his low price had just blown my mind. It was almost half the price I'd paid in the past.

"I'll take it," I replied, not saying another word.

Doug appeared to be the type of guy who'd sell to anyone. He was a small-time dealer, the type every town in America has. They're easy to pick out because their homes usually have abnormal volumes of traffic, coming and going at odd hours, for short visits. They're different from the large-scale dealers, because large-scale dealers only deal with select individuals, and usually own legitimate businesses, in case they ever need to pass an IRS Lifestyle Audit. Despite that, I've found that all drug dealers have one thing in common . . . they want to level up from their current social class. Some dealers want to put more food on the table, some want the freshest sneakers on the block, and some want the biggest and best of everything. Only a few do it for the thrill. I suppose you could say a drug dealer's life can be summed up as: It didn't go as planned, but it's all good.

After Doug pushed himself up from the sofa, he led us into a bedroom where he weighed out my ounce and said, "Come over anytime. I'm always open for business," and that's exactly what I ended up doing.

I continued scoring with Doug into my senior year and settled into a groove of distributing two to three ounces a month, which netted me a couple hundred bucks and free weed to get me and my close buddies high after school. My routine was like clockwork: inhale the good shit, exhale the bullshit, and be home in time to study and maintain my recent and decent satisfactory grade point average.

It wasn't just my acceptable grades that loosened my noose. I had also received an acceptance letter from Plattsburgh State University of New York, and Mom was ecstatic. I was too, because I felt like it was the first time she was proud of me, and it also granted me the freedom to cruise around town aimlessly with my buddies, while smoking joints and laughing about nothing. I suppose you could say I was bonding, and my favorite pastime with them was buying whatever food I wanted, without having to look at the price tag.

"WHO WANTS TACO BELL?" a buddy shouted back to a bunch of us from the front seat of his Chevy Suburban one afternoon.

"Hell, yes!" we all shouted from different rows of the vehicle, through a cloud of smoke.

When we pulled up to the drive-thru, I could see the Chicken Chalupas on the menu. They were $1.29 each and looked delicious. I'd been waiting to try them for years, but whenever Mom bought us Taco Bell on a road trip, she always said she didn't have coupons for the speciality items. But now with my disposable income, I could happily order three Chalupas, and I did, because I felt rich. I felt rich because I had options, and I liked having options because it meant I was in control of my life. And I definitely liked having control, because subconsciously it made me feel like I'd survive. I've learned there's a trick, though, and that's to avoid wanting to control everything, because whenever you control everything you can't enjoy anything.

As we pulled away from the drive-thru window, my stoner

buddies passed back my order between blasts of laughter. I couldn't wait to unwrap the Chalupas, and when we pulled into a parking spot, I climbed out of the cargo area, shook out my legs, and walked higher than Cheech and Chong to sit and eat on the curb.

The first Chalupa bite was like heaven. No pain, no discomfort, and no emotional lows. I felt grateful—everything around me felt light—and the Chalupas tasted as good as they looked. I was finally living the life I'd waited for. Buying my own meal, with my own money, was true freedom. It wasn't just about the tasty food; it was also about the peacefulness. I didn't have to wolf food down while watching for flailing hands or fielding criticisms. Instead, I had time to savor each bite, and I felt like a winner, and it wasn't luck. It was years of big dreams combined with determination—something more potent than making honor roll.

7

REPUTATION

I'm happy to say, I made it to 1997 and Mom was excited to be driving me to Plattsburgh, New York, to begin my Business Management Degree. I only had $540 in my debit account for "extracurricular activities," but thankfully I had successfully smuggled a couple ounces of organic, sparkly bud in the car with us, inside two boxes of dryer sheets I'd cut open with a razor blade and sealed shut with superglue.

I didn't intend to sell the weed in college, but after smoking it with some newfound friends on campus, it took only a month for word to spread that "Lips has the best weed around," and by the fourth week into the semester, I had broken down and created a delivery service that provided weed at any time, at a fair price, and at the correct weight.

I still attended all my classes, but when class was finished, I would rush back to my dorm room to check for my customer orders that were either left on my dry-erase board hanging on my door or my college-issued answering machine. The messages were always left in code, and once I deciphered the amount the customers wanted, I'd prepare their orders, and begin my delivery route on an old classic Schwinn I'd bought at a garage sale for $20, selling bags of grass out of my backpack as I cruised late into the night.

I'd sell to foreign exchange students, girls in glasses playing Scrabble, Phish Heads jamming on steel drums, and gym rats looking for their next buzz. It was a business that I ran twenty-four-seven to build a solid reputation that people would remember. I saw keg parties, dance parties, coke parties, and dope parties. I also saw the video gamers and study groups, and within a year I was doing close to $50,000 a month in sales.

I bought my bulk weed from a few different Plattsburgh townies I'd met through mutual friends. They were safe connections, and I always showed up to my customers' homes with a positive energy that introduced me before I spoke. I promoted trust, passed a few laughs, and had a quick superficial conversation while keeping one eye on my watch for the next delivery. Customers often invited me to smoke with them, and many offered other drugs too: mushrooms, coke, quaaludes, valium, acid . . . and since they all sounded interesting, my default reply usually was, "I'll try it." I'd then quickly swallow, smoke, or snort anything they had, before exiting their residence. It was a fascinating and blurry time, but it didn't take long for the lifestyle to drain me. So much so that I decided to quit smoking weed, hoping I'd have more energy. I didn't quit the other drugs, though, because they gave me a temporary cheek-to-cheek smile, which became my trademark and helped my business flourish. They also excused me from real conversations. Ones that could reveal an embarrassing truth: I'd never had sex.

AFTER MAKING my rounds one night, I headed to my usual last stop at my buddy Rob's, who majored in business management, and whom I paid to highlight the important stuff in my textbooks for my review prior to exams. I also paid him to use his place as a stash house for my weed, because keeping it in my dorm room was too risky. Rob was trustworthy, an expert back-country skier, and the perfect accomplice, because he was unassuming. He was about average height and clean-cut and wore T-shirts, corduroys, and Saucony running shoes. Like me, he wasn't flashy, and most importantly, if anyone asked him questions about me, he'd surely play deaf.

Rob lived off-campus with a couple of chill roommates. One of his roommates was from Venezuela and the head of our study abroad program. He was a computer wiz, and as I approached his house from half a block away, I could hear the bass from his stereo playing some groovy Latin music.

Frustration immediately hit me, because I knew that any abnormal activity at the house could've brought unwanted attention toward my operation. But when I opened their front door, my mood pleasantly changed to the sight of at least a dozen beautiful South American women salsa dancing under the faint glow of Christmas lights. Blaring music, laughter, smoke, and perfume filled the air of the tiny living room, which was decorated with tapestries on the walls, lava lamps on the shelves, bongs on the tables, and a guitar next to the couch. The scene looked like an MTV video. All the women were dressed in either short, tight, backless dresses or tiny halter tops with perfectly positioned push-up bras. Compared to the rest of the girls on campus, they were in another league.

As I squeezed my way through the women's swaying curves, I could tell they didn't know the semiotics of American culture. They couldn't have cared less where I grew up, what kind of car I drove, or what brand of clothes I was wearing. To them I was just a guy, either handsome or not.

While the women sang along in Spanish, I couldn't understand anything except, "Mi amor," and when one of them pinched my arm—I turned around to see Sofia—a girl I'd briefly met at a previous party, who knew some broken English. Sofia was tall and voluptuous, with long, silky black hair. She motioned for me to dance with her, but I needed to stash my backpack full of weed in one of the back rooms first.

When I came back into the party area, I sat on the couch, hoping to sober up from my rounds. While sitting, I maintained eye contact with Sofia, as she continued her sultry dance behind a girl who was dancing on a coffee table directly in front of me. That's when it hit me—Sofia was going to be my first. She didn't need to know my story or get confirmation from her friends that I was cool enough to sleep with. I could've just given her the raw truth and said, "My name's Eric, and I sell weed because I never want to be trapped again. Do you want to get out of here?" and she still would've jumped on me like I hit the lottery.

Once I determined my chances of rejection were minimal, I stood up and walked toward Sofia on the dance floor. With a bravado I didn't know I possessed, I put my hands on her hips, synced my steps up to hers, and whispered in her ear, "I like your lips," and within seconds, Sofia grabbed the back of my head and pressed a deep kiss on me. I could feel the kiss run straight down my spine, through my heart, and into my balls quicker than lightning. It was an unfamiliar feeling, and I liked it. It saved me from a lot of talking.

It didn't take long for Sofia to pull me by my hand to a vacant back bedroom, and as we entered the dark room, I became nervous. She smiled, though, which gave me assurance as she pulled off my shirt, her shirt, and her jeans.

I was in unknown territory, but I wasn't afraid to navigate it wrong, because I assumed word of my inexperience wouldn't spread far in Spanish. Plus, she was flying back to Argentina in a week anyway, so it was an opportune time for me to practice what I'd seen in the movies: one kiss, two fingers, and a few thrusts.

I know I wasn't a rock star, but we did it, and afterward, Sofia fell asleep with her head on my chest as I thought to myself, *This is what life's about.*

Yeah, I was awkward in bed. I felt I was on stage, being reviewed and graded. Graded on a role I'd never rehearsed. I wanted to do it properly, but the stage fright was intense. I felt overtaxed by worry and pressure. So taxed that I couldn't be my true self. The truth was, I just wanted to take things slow. I wanted to unwind and lounge skin-to-skin. I wanted to warm up, but there was another part of me that didn't want to let Sofia down or fail her expectations—even though I made most of them up in my head. I have an excuse, though—the movies—ones that had perpetuated a fairy tale in my mind that sex was a sequence of events I had to follow, and if I didn't follow them correctly, I was doing it wrong and would be labeled as: "He's weird."

8

SUPPLY AND DEMAND

By senior year, I'd broken Plattsburgh up into territories and had select weed distributors living in each one. I also had access to several wholesale suppliers located in neighboring towns along the Canadian border, who had the infrastructure to smuggle Canadian weed into the United States. My network was tight, and my associates respected me because I never ran my mouth, I always under-promised and over-delivered, and I always thought ahead. But none of my associates knew I had thought to triple-seal and bury over $100,000 in the Adirondacks to pay for a criminal attorney, because none of them knew Mom, who trained me to prepare for the worst.

I had one other tool to further my operation—Grandma's old 1987 Pontiac Bonneville—a gift that assisted me in getting to my out-of-town meetings so I no longer had to rent friends' cars. The Bonneville was well maintained and inconspicuous, which helped me blend in, despite the fact that I was the number one marijuana dealer for my college. It took me three years to gain that title, but after I'd built relationships based on trust, that trust drove my revenue close to $150,000 per month.

. . .

SIX MONTHS AWAY FROM GRADUATION, on a gray Monday in November, I saw the headline in the local paper: "Cocaine Ring Busted."

I froze. Of course I knew all the players.

My mind started spinning. . . . *Is Kurt going to rat everyone out? How much do they know? Did Mick get busted too? Is the twenty grand Mick owes me safe?* I wanted answers.

Mick had been a customer of mine who kept pressing me to meet his coke dealer, Kurt, who often wanted my weed on consignment to bring to NYC and sell. Kurt was flashy. Crisp attire, spiked hair with gel, and a Lexus with shiny rims. I wasn't interested in meeting him, though, because cocaine attracts a lot of heat, due to its high profit margins. That's why I only sold weed, because the margins in weed were minimal due to industry saturation. Even when everything went perfectly for me, which it rarely did, I barely netted ten percent. That's why law enforcement put minimal effort into tracking weed dealers, unless they heard it was a big operation. And I never let anyone know the size of my operation, because secrets are rarely kept— not unless someone's dead.

As I rushed to Mick's apartment, I prepared to hear he'd given my weed to Kurt and it'd been confiscated in the bust. And sure enough, when Mick's roommate answered the door, I could see the gloom in his face, which told me the DEA had raided their apartment, too.

"I gotta come in," I said, not waiting for permission.

"You can check," the roommate said as I brushed past. "But everything's gone. They searched the place top to bottom and took Mick away in cuffs last night."

Apparently, Mick had been storing a kilo of coke for Kurt, which the DEA had seized, and I assumed they'd taken my money, too, but I needed to see for myself.

I attempted to search, but I gave up as I walked down their

narrow hallway and saw each room had been turned upside down. I now knew it was just a matter of time before they'd come for me. I had to prepare.

While walking back to my house, part of me was afraid and part of me was excited. *Who's going to win?* I thought. Do they have enough evidence on me? Will Mick keep his mouth shut? How will they piece my network together? I knew, though, they wouldn't. Why? Because I'd always kept everyone in my network separate, and I ran my entire life on a need-to-know basis. I never exposed my private life; that would've only left me open to attack.

The next week was a blur, and by my fifth sleepless night in a row, I decided the DEA would already have come for me if they'd had a solid case. The smart money said to close up shop, but it wasn't that easy. My business was a living entity, with my money in many different customers' hands at any given time. I couldn't just say, "Hey, the DEA is onto me. I need you to quickly sell the rest of the weed I gave you and pay me back." No, my customers expected to be replenished with weed every time I came to collect my money. It was an unspoken responsibility of mine, because they counted on me to maintain the lifestyle they'd become accustomed to. And I felt obligated, because I couldn't have made it without them. They stuck with me, even when they had windows to score product from other sources at lower prices. We were a team, something I had wanted to be a part of all my life. Plus, I had inventory at Rob's, and I couldn't just return it with a receipt and I wasn't about to burn it. It all needed to be sold, more discreetly than ever. So that's what I did, because my success was based on my ability to find solutions.

A WEEK LATER, I was at my house watching the movie *Office Space* and Mick showed up out of the blue. He was out of jail, which meant one of two things: he was either waiting for trial or working for the DEA. Either way, I was glad to see him, because waiting around to find out what the Feds did or didn't know had my nerves fraying.

"Yo . . . waz up, brother?" I asked, pretending to be happy to see Mick as he came through my front door.

"Yo," he replied, nodding his head and taking a seat on my couch. When he leaned back, he didn't make eye contact—he just stared at my TV. He looked rough, with bloodshot eyes and a pale face, as he said, "I lined up a good deal. I have a guy who wants a hundred pounds."

Ding! Ding! Ding! Right then, I knew he was wearing a wire. He and I both knew I didn't do deals that big. Plus, no small talk? He just jumped straight to business? This red flag was good news, because it confirmed the cops didn't have solid evidence against me and were trying to get some right then and there, which I wasn't going to give.

I sat straight up from my slump on the couch. "What are you talking about?" I said, knowing that someone, somewhere was listening. "Have you been skiing yet?" I added, trying to buy some time while I grabbed a pen and paper. I'd also been rehearsing for this conversation all week.

"No, the mountain's not open yet," he replied.

"I heard they're getting dumped on up there."

Mick murmured in agreement, doing his job for the DEA. I could tell they'd brainwashed him for this conversation.

"They'll be open soon," I said, keeping the small talk going, as I wrote on a piece of paper: *I know you're wearing a wire; tell me what they want; I won't blow your cover.* I then held my right index finger to my lips, and handed him the paper and pen with my left hand as I stood up and said, "Hold on, I gotta use the bathroom."

I wanted to give Mick time to write back without making the

DEA suspicious of our dead air time. It was imperative that the DEA felt like they were in control, because if they knew I was "onto" them, they'd quickly turn up the heat.

When I returned to the family room, Mick's eyes were closed and he was leaning back into the couch cushion. I could see desperation in his face as he handed me a piece of paper with the words: *"They call you "Slick." They think you're the financial backer."*

I slowly took in the confirmation that they wanted my money, and for a second I was proud of my accomplishment. I felt important. I liked my nickname, too, and Mick was starting to make a good double agent. But part of me felt sorry for him. He was trapped. The DEA probably told him he'd get off with a slap on the wrist if he brought me down.

"Were you at Rob's party last week?" I asked, while writing: *How much do they think I have?*

"Yeah, it was bumpin'," he replied, while he wrote: *80k.*

I kept up the chatter about Rob's party as I wrote back: *Tell them I'm broke and out of the game. Where's my money?*

Mick wrote back: *I gave the weed to Kurt. He traded it for the coke, and the DEA seized it. Your money's gone. They bugged Kurt's house and heard people talking about "Lips." They know about you. Be careful.*

I quickly accepted the loss, because the intel Mick provided was giving me an edge over the enemy.

As Mick stood up to leave, I burned the paper we were writing on over an ashtray and I invited him to Rob's next party. I wanted to keep tabs on him. He was my line to the government.

I was happy to find the DEA didn't know I was worth around a quarter-million between my working capital and what I had buried, and knowing that, I assumed they wouldn't waste a lot of resources on me. They had bigger fish to fry. I was just a small potential bonus at the end of their coke bust. Even so, I had to presume my home phone was tapped, because that was an inexpensive operation they could've managed from their headquarters, so I stopped taking calls on it. I also checked my car for tracking devices at a do-it-yourself car wash. I even took a couple dry runs to see if I was being tailed. I made sure I kept my home trash cans clean, too. No baggies, ledgers, or debris associated with marijuana at all.

I hoped my discretion would give me the benefit of the doubt.

IT WAS A SATURDAY, about three weeks into the investigation, and two of my housemates wanted to go for a hike in the Adirondacks. I told them I was in, because I figured the woods would recenter me—which I needed now more than ever—since I hadn't seen Mick in a couple weeks, and couldn't stop thinking about if and when the DEA would strike again.

We took my Bonneville, which was good, because I wanted to see if anyone was following us as we drove out of town.

"Lips, you okay, buddy?" Rob, who was now one of my roommates, asked from the back seat.

"The government is investigating me and our house is probably bugged," I wanted to reply, but I didn't. I hadn't told anyone that Mick had flipped. That would've just driven the DEA further underground. My safest bet was to continue acting oblivious to the investigation.

"All's good. I'm just thinking about this chick I met in Econ class," I lied.

"Bitches. This'll help," Rob replied, holding up a bag of psychedelic mushrooms over my shoulder, near my face. "Have some!"

They looked tempting. Shrooms were the one drug that gave me a higher understanding of both my environment and myself.

They were therapeutic, too. So after we made it a few miles out of town and I hadn't seen anything suspicious in the rearview, I willingly ate a handful of them.

Unfortunately, the shrooms' life-altering power started kicking in before we parked, and I suddenly felt trapped. I could feel the seat belt cutting into my chest and the windshield felt overwhelmingly close. I wanted to pull over, and run off into the woods. Not just that . . . I wanted out of Plattsburgh, out of my house, and out of the game. But I didn't pull over; I just continued driving down the windy road with my foot light on the gas as a kaleidoscope of government agents paraded through my mind, chanting, "We got him!"

"Lips, relax, buddy. We're almost there," Rob laughed, as I stirred in my seat.

The minute we pulled into the trailhead parking lot, I shot out of the car, ran to the nearest tree, and hauled myself up into it like a wild animal. As I touched my face against the trees' bark, I could feel its calm pulse and I took a breath with it. I felt safe for the first time in weeks. There were no cameras or wire-taps here, because nature never failed me—it was my home.

Rob yelled to me, but I couldn't make out what he and Jay were saying. They were translucent by now, and as the mush-rooms pushed their magic further into my veins, I jumped out of the tree, landed on all fours like a cat, and grabbed my keys out of the ignition as Jay handed me my jacket, before I bolted toward the trailhead.

While wandering ahead of Rob and Jay, I could feel the dry fall leaves crunching under my feet, and after about ten minutes of navigating up the rocky trail, I heard the sound of running water, and a tingle ran through me.

I wanted to find the source of the sound, so I bushwhacked a short stretch through the woods, and soon found myself standing at the edge of a brook, where water eddied around rocks, creating small whirlpools. I could faintly hear Rob and Jay behind me, but I didn't turn around. Instead, I turned my head upward and saw one snowflake floating down from above, perhaps the first one of the season. I watched it drift past my face, land in the stream, and then melt and disappear, rejoining the very thing that made it. It was the most beautiful art I'd ever seen. It was perfection.

I closed my eyes and surrendered, as a deep vision formed just across from me, on the other side of the stream. It was a small, sturdy man who walked out of the woods and stepped onto a large boulder. He had on a sarong of some sort. His skin was grooved, his eyes were dark and furrowed, and his face was welcoming. He looked like a guy I'd seen on the cover of one of Mom's *National Geographic* magazines she left in the bathroom for her guests.

"Stay here," the man said. "This is where you belong. Everything you need to live is right here. Stay . . ."

I was speechless, but eventually I replied, "I will." I then blinked, and the vision was gone. "Stay here," I mumbled. Then louder, I shouted, "I'm gonna stay here!"

"What, Lips?" asked Rob, who was now standing on the bank next to me.

"I'm going to live here," I replied in victory.

Rob and Jay were tripping their faces off, too, and all three of us were silent for a moment, before Rob replied, "We'll stay, too."

They didn't know what I saw, but Rob wouldn't leave me behind. He was the type of friend who would not only eat with me, but would also starve with me.

"I'm not going back. I'm going to build a house here," I said softly.

Rob and Jay appeared miles away, so I wasn't sure if they'd

heard me. And as I closed my eyes, a new image appeared—my lawyer money—buried underground, rotting away.

I held the image, mesmerized, as a voice in my head said, "You don't need it."

Still standing in silence, I reflected, and I started thinking things through. I reasoned that I just needed to build a fort to sleep in, a slingshot to hunt with, and a fire to cook on. And as my plan started taking shape, I crouched down and clawed my hands deep into the streambed, grabbing pebbles and sand.

As I washed my hands with the earth, the silt felt real—better than any dollar I'd ever touched. Then the voice came back. "Your money owns you. You think you own it, but it owns your soul. Give it all away."

Right then, I was done . . . I was out of the game. I didn't want my money, and I didn't want the stress. I wanted to stay at the stream forever, because nature was my doctor.

"Lips, let's go," Jay urged.

"Wait," I replied.

They both stopped and turned to look at me. It took me a minute to collect my thoughts, but I spit it out. "I have some money. I need you guys to take it and give it to my mom. It's killing me."

They stared at me, and then Jay started laughing and laughing. And then so did Rob. They both knew I sold enough weed to get a Texas marching band high.

"Why give it away, Lips? Let's spend it!" Jay said. "Let's go back to the car, drive up to Montreal, and get some hookers."

"Yes . . . ," I said slowly, trailing back into reality.

ON OUR DRIVE back to civilization I could feel my mind coming back, processing the day.

Those shrooms were no joke. They showed me my flaws. They helped me recognize the bond I had with Mom. They showed me I'd do anything to win her over. But the thought of giving her money was more about me, not her. I felt if I gave her money, she'd be proud of me. Like all her strict rules paid off, but I was torn, because pleasing her may have been a never-ending feat. So when I didn't take the turn directing us to Canada, Rob and Jay sensed money-hungry Eric was back, and they settled for me buying them dinner in Plattsburgh—a place where I could reset and refocus.

There was no way I was ready to quit dealing. It was the only thing I was good at. Plus, it was the week before Winter Break, the biggest weed sales week of the year. It was the week I'd get slammed with orders because everyone wanted weed to share at their upcoming holiday parties. The problem was, my inventory was low—and if I couldn't fill orders before kids left town for break, I'd feel like a failure. So I had to restock somehow, even though it felt unsafe, because I still wasn't sure who the rat was that'd brought Kurt and Mick down. I suspected he was still lurking around Plattsburgh as a government informant, which meant my only option was to get weed from one of my distant suppliers. One outside of the imaginary jurisdiction I'd created for the Plattsburgh DEA.

I had several connections along the Canadian border, including some bikers in Vermont as well as a couple others who lived on the Mohawk Reservation. I liked the idea of purchasing from the reservation because the Mohawk tribe is considered a sovereign nation in many ways, and it prohibits federal and state officials from patrolling the stretch of the St. Lawrence River that runs within their land along the Canadian border. This made the reservation ripe for smuggling weed, immigrants, coke, guns, and cigarettes. And knowing this, it seemed to be the safest source for my last run of the year, so I decided to use a pay phone outside of town to set up a meeting with one of my Native American connections, named Etu, who lived an hour and a half away from Plattsburgh.

LATER THAT EVENING, I pulled into Etu's secluded driveway right on time. It was actually the first time I'd been to his personal residence. Usually, our meetings took place at one of his stash houses, where he regularly rattled my nerves when he spoke of his piranha fish tank and coke habit. I think it was his way of letting me know everyone pays their tab one way or another.

Etu was running late, so I turned on my dome light and opened my microeconomics book, figuring I'd use the time to brush up on the law of supply and demand before my final exam, the following morning. The law was common sense to me, and the reason my weed prices were the most competitive in the market.

As the quiet night settled around my car, Etu eventually pulled up in his shiny new Lincoln Navigator, and when he hopped out of it, he smiled, and a black hole formed in his mouth from too many missing teeth. I'm not sure why he was missing teeth, and I never asked, even though he smiled a lot. I just knew he was short and wiry, mid-thirties, had a black mullet, and always had on the same outfit, which consisted of a flannel, jeans, and steel-toed work boots. I also knew we both cheated the system for the same exact reason: because we were more focused on what was missing in our lives, rather than what it had.

When Etu motioned for me to follow him into his three-bay garage attached to his house, I stepped out of the Bonneville, exchanged a cheerful "Howdy" with him, and followed him and his footprints in the fresh dusting of snow.

Once we made it into the side entrance of the garage, Etu flipped on a light and the first thing I saw was a classic red

Mustang, in mint condition. In the farthest bay, I could see a late-model black Chevy pickup. And in the middle bay were his three shiny Harleys, with just enough room in front of them for a workbench, snug against the back wall, with a single fluorescent bulb hanging overhead. I wanted to ask questions, but I didn't, because I knew Etu trusted actions more than words.

As Etu led me over to the workbench, I could see a bunch of greasy tools and two semi-automatic rifles resting among boxes of ammo. I pretended not to notice the guns and ammo, but I had nothing to fear because I always kept my word, and my business was a sport, not a war.

While Etu grabbed a lighter off the workbench and lit a smoke, I realized a million little choices had brought me eye to eye with a real drug dealer. They hadn't felt like choices at the time, though, because I had shot out of Mom's house faster than a cannonball and landed here, making felonious arrangements as chained pit bulls whined outside.

"So are you ready to take some work, my friend?" Etu asked, turning his attention to me, as he exhaled a plume of smoke.

I looked Etu dead in the eye and replied, "I think so, but I didn't want to tell you over the phone—there's been a lot of heat in Plattsburgh lately."

"Come on, buddy . . . there's always heat. No one said it was gonna be easy," he said, flashing a black smile my way.

"This is different. My name came up in an investigation and it's been near impossible to work since," I said, seeking his advice.

"Impossible? That just means you haven't found the right solution," Etu chuckled. "Trust me. . . if they're askin' questions, they have nothing. Remember, it ain't over 'til it's over."

Etu's lack of fear reminded me how reckless he was, but it calmed me at the same time. I felt safe in his fortress, and for a moment, I felt like he was more powerful than the law.

As Etu took another drag on his smoke, he left it dangling between his three or so teeth, as he walked toward his Chevy, leaned inside, and turned the ignition key one click forward. He then pulled what looked like a credit card from his pocket and swiped it into the groove where the windshield and the roof met, while holding down a button on the stereo in the dash. I immediately heard the sound of a hydraulic motor whirring, and turned my head to see the back bumper of the truck descending. The bumper eventually stopped lowering after about eight inches, and when I stepped closer to it, I saw a piece of sheet metal behind where the bumper was originally located.

A second later, Etu walked around back next to me, slid off the sheet metal, and revealed a six-inch-tall compartment that ran under the entire bed of the truck.

"Nothing's impossible," Etu said, looking like a little boy showing off his Lego project. His eyes looked like they were twinkling, and I played it cool, even though it was the most badass thing I'd ever seen—a false bottom—in the underbelly of the Chevy.

Etu put gloves on, bent over, and shined a flashlight deep into the hidden compartment. Inside were bags and bags of weed. It was a beautiful sight.

"Put these on," Etu said, handing me a pair of work gloves.

I slipped the gloves on, knowing our fingerprints shouldn't be on the bags. Etu then pulled out a pound of weed from the hidden compartment. The weed was sealed in an airtight freezer bag and looked spectacular, but I couldn't stop staring at the truck. I wanted one. The contraption was ingenious.

"Did you build this?" I asked.

"No, I have a shop that builds secret compartments in any vehicle," he replied. "This one cost 30k. You want one?"

I did want one, but I replied, "Maybe someday," knowing this could be my last deal.

In the immediate moment, I just wanted this particular batch of weed, so I asked: "Can you deliver thirty pounds of this weed to me next week?"

"Yes, sir!"

"Perfect! Here's the drop point," I replied, handing him a piece of paper from my chest pocket with the address of a friend's house in Plattsburgh, which had a detached garage where I could discreetly unload the truck.

After Etu stuffed the piece of paper into his pocket, he pulled a dollar bill out of his other pocket and ripped it in half, before handing me one of the two pieces.

"What's this?" I asked.

"Hold onto that half. When my driver arrives, don't talk to him. Just make sure the serial number on his half matches the serial number on your half. If not, you'll be meeting the wrong guy . . . got it?"

"Got it," I replied, sliding my half into my wallet as we walked out of the garage.

Once we were back out in Etu's driveway, he said, "You should get a beeper or a celly."

I looked at him, thinking, knowing no one had a cell phone in college. I then looked at my textbooks on the passenger seat of the Bonneville and replied with a smile, "Then I'll look like a drug dealer."

Etu laughed, as I added, "Don't forget, I'm just a student with a dream."

Etu smiled and replied, "Dream big then, buddy. If we build in silence, they won't know what to attack."

Etu was a purebred outlaw, and it brought an additional level of uncertainty and danger to the addictive game, and not knowing when "Game Over" would be called kept me advancing into more unknown territories—for more rewards—ones in the form of cold, hard cash that allowed me to manifest almost any experience I wanted.

I think for me, subconsciously, money was a form of mood management. It allowed me to buy whatever I wanted, which allowed me to converse about the things I had, rather than the person I was. It also allowed me to pay for everyone's food and drinks around me. Money was the best drug, and I think paying was my way of being accepted. It's how I fit in, and I'm embarrassed to say, I was addicted to money, because I couldn't fathom how others would perceive me if I no longer had it. It felt good to hear someone say, "Thanks for dinner," or, "I like your new bike," or, "Nice jacket." Compliments fueled me. I think they fuel everyone, and advertisers know this. They know exactly how to tap into our insecurities. They know what we need to feel better about ourselves, and these advertisers tug on our heartstrings every day, because that's what they're trained to do and that's what good ads are supposed to do. It's basic marketing. And I've noticed ads are everywhere I look, except in nature—the place of truth—and the place where everything seems to make sense.

9

SAFETY

The following week, Etu's driver showed up at my buddy's garage, right on time. After I'd successfully matched my half of the dollar bill to the driver's half, we unloaded the truck's secret compartment as I heard Jim's voice echoing in my head, "Shut your mouth, and do your work." And that's exactly what I did; I kept all my next moves to myself as I delivered ten pounds on foot, unannounced, to four different local customers—with my head on a swivel the entire time, checking for surveillance. I left the other twenty pounds stashed under a tarp in the corner of the garage. I intended to drive it to Lake George after exam week, before heading to Mom's for Winter Break. The break I needed.

CAMPUS WAS a ghost town on the last day of exams. The majority of students had left town early, due to a nasty storm heading our way. My roommates had left, too, and when the blizzard started around 3 p.m., it showed no sign of letting up. Thankfully, I had planned ahead and safely transferred the twenty pounds to the trunk of my

Bonneville the night before. I also made sure I had a full tank of gas and that my bags were packed. I had one problem, though. When I was ready to hit the snow-covered roads, I couldn't, because when I peeked out the window of my house, there was an Impala parked at the end of the street, about ten houses down. I could see the exhaust curling out of its tailpipe and drifting up into the cold air, which meant the car was on and someone was in it. I knew it was an undercover agent, running the engine for heat.

I was a sitting duck. Mick must've told them my primary business was out-of-town deliveries, which it was, so this is when they planned to roadkill me—that is, conveniently pull me over for "failing to obey a traffic device"—then search my car under the probable cause that they "smelled marijuana." It's a bullshit trap, but one that's commonly used.

As the day faded to night, I peaked out the window every twenty minutes or so and realized I was in a standoff, with no clean way out. My only sensible option was to try and sleep. So I crawled into bed and pulled the comforter over me as snow quietly piled up outside my window. It was an eerie feeling, but at least I felt comfort in knowing that none of my peers were around to see me get handcuffed, because failure in front of others was one of my biggest fears. It was my fear of shame. Fuck, I never forgot how hard it was to make friends when I was considered a loser.

AROUND 9 P.M., I started to form an idea that could potentially help me escape and deliver to my Lake George customer. I could call my customer from my home phone, which was definitely tapped, and create a false trail for the DEA.

"Hello!" my customer answered.

"Yo! Quick update . . . I'm not going to make it tonight.

There's a blizzard up here. I won't be able to leave for another day or two," I said.

"There's one here, too. Take your time. There's no rush."

"Coolio, I'm going to pass out. I'll call you tomorrow afternoon and update you on the weather."

I hung up with a proper farewell and turned off all the lights in the house. I then got back in bed and waited. I had no idea how phone taps worked. Did they hear me immediately or was there a delay? If they heard it immediately, there was no reason for them to sit outside all night in the cold and watch my house while I slept. That would've been a waste of time. Plus, if there was a bug in my house, they'd surely assume I was asleep, so that they could leave and come back in the morning.

An hour later I tiptoed to the window, and the Impala was gone. My heart started pounding. It felt almost too good to be true, but my plan had worked. The only car in the vicinity was my trusty Bonneville, parked in the driveway.

It was now or never, so I grabbed my duffel bag of clothes and walked out the back door, like a robot on autopilot. No thoughts, just action. I had to force myself to be slow and deliberate, even though I wanted to run.

After I locked the house door with steady hands, I got in my car, threw my duffel in the back seat, and slowly reversed. The Bonneville was a tank. I knew it could handle the snow. It probably weighed two tons. Plus, Jim had taught me how to handle a car in the snow when we used to do donuts in the back of the shopping center parking lots, while waiting for Mom to come out of stores with *stuff*. Which was always frustrating, because I hated watching Mom walk toward the car with tchotchkes, right after complaining about not having enough money.

I drove to the end of the street and made a full stop at the stop sign. I properly used my turn signal and checked the rearview. No one was there, so I took the turn and drove several miles below the speed limit. I didn't have any music on; the only sounds were those of my front defroster blasting through the car and my heart hammering against my chest. The Bonneville felt like a ship, one I was steering down the unplowed streets, past the darkened houses and closed stores. I only had to drive three miles to reach the interstate, and once I had merged on, my heart was less jumpy.

It was a complete whiteout on the interstate. I felt like I was in a snow globe, and after I'd made it over ten miles—in tunnel vision—I still didn't have any tails. The only vehicles I saw were a couple stranded in a snowbank, which comforted me, because I knew the cops would be assisting those drivers and not looking to pull over a Bonneville with all its lights working properly and staying within the wind-blown tire tracks.

After twenty miles, I allowed myself to smile a little, and soon after I broke into a wide grin as I slammed my fist down on the dash and screamed, "Fuck yeah! Merry Christmas!"

I couldn't believe it, but I was in the clear. I was a fuckin' magician, and I would deliver as promised, like I always had, because like Jim told me, "If you can't keep your word, you'll lose credibility." And those words from Jim had always remained with me, because credibility was currency. When I said things once, people believed me. And in celebration of this—I turned the heat up, cracked the windows open, and popped a Bob Marley MiniDisc in my aftermarket deck—and started jamming to "Three Little Birds."

"*Every little thing, is gonna be alright...*" I sang along as the snow came down thicker than a blanket. I assumed other parts of the world were probably at home with their loved ones, wrapping presents and drinking eggnog, but I was having my own private party, right there in the Bonneville, with Bob Marley and $78,000 worth of grass.

"That's why they call you 'Slick!'" I screamed over the music, giving the dashboard a few more love taps. That's when it hit me: It wasn't just about the money—it was about the thrill. I'd beaten The Man. I'd beaten the house. And I did it with skill—not skill that I was born with, but skill that I was learning through experience. I was becoming an expert drug dealer. Why? Because I understood both sides of the law.

I ENDED up arriving at my buddy's house around midnight, and he was still awake, drinking whiskey around his Christmas tree with friends and beyond happy to see me. "Look who it is! Fucking Santa Claus!" he said, giving me a jolly old hug. If he only knew what I'd just been through, I thought, but I didn't say a word. I didn't want anything to dampen this victorious day because I'd won and I wanted to soak it up. However, I must credit Mom for the win, because she trained me to stay flexible in life. She did it by having me make long to-do lists, and then when she made me rework those lists she would say: "Change is the only constant in life, Eric. You better adapt with it. If not, you better be willing to lose."

IT WAS AROUND 1 a.m. when I pulled into Mom's driveway for Winter Break. I could see her friend's snow-covered car in the driveway and Christmas tree lights on in the family room. Mom loved having people over throughout the holidays. She always did a great job decorating the house with fresh-cut wreaths, tinsel, bows, ornaments, and a wall plastered with holiday cards from friends and family. I think the cards made her feel loved. She used to say, "Look how many friends I have." I didn't understand why she'd say that every year, but I get it now. I think it was her form of verifying that other people liked her. I suppose we all have our own way of keeping track of who likes us. That's probably why Facebook displays our friends count. I think they do it so we'll come back for more. One more "like," one more "friend," and one more hit of external validation.

Mom must have heard me rummaging in the garage for a spot to temporarily hide the $80,000 I had on me, because she surprised me when she entered the garage from the main house and shouted: "Merry Christmas, Eric!"

Mom was happier than ever to see me. Every time I successfully completed a semester, she became more ecstatic, because receiving my diploma became more of a sure bet.

"Merry Christmas, Mom!" I replied, walking from the corner of the garage, where I'd just finished stashing my cash under her garden tools before she had noticed.

"Did you like my care package?" she asked, open-armed.

"Yes, thank you. I left a message on your answering machine, saying the food was delicious!" I answered, giving her a deep hug.

I'd never felt so *safe* in Mom's arms before. She worried about me. Maybe she'd even protect me from the DEA, I thought. Actually, I didn't know how she would react if she'd known I'd broken the law. I just assumed it was best that she knew nothing, because I liked our new relationship, and her house finally felt like a safe place to go to in an emergency.

10

GROWTH

I was off the DEA's radar by the time I returned to Plattsburgh. They had bigger fish to fry, which meant I could graduate on time with a clean record in order to start my new life in historic Saratoga Springs, New York, as Eric Canori the Pond Guy.

Between Mom asking me what I was going to do for a career and the vision at the stream advising me to remain close to nature, I'd decided to start a small company designing and installing ponds, streams, and waterfalls. I had acquired the idea from a high school friend, who gave me a pamphlet promoting how to build a business in the water feature industry. The business allowed me to be a law-abiding citizen by day, but at night things were different. I felt safe in the peaceful Saratoga. It was the perfect hub for my expanding weed business. It was a tiny city, had low crime with minimal law enforcement, and it was 150 miles away from the Canadian border—just far enough away from the DEA's immediate border scrutiny but still close enough to work it.

I had a simple strategy to stay off the DEA's radar in my new hometown—never deal with locals, only with discreet out-of-town players. Creating distance between me and my customers would be just one more obstacle for any potential DEA investigation to shut me down. And none of my pond customers had a clue that my main source of income was from weed, because I created a persona that made it a challenge for anyone to figure out my reality, including myself. Publicly, I was a tax-paying citizen. But privately, I was an outlaw.

I enjoyed bringing peace and harmony into families' backyards. I'd often lose track of time while working with my hands in the dirt and water. I had a good eye for design, too. My work was showcased in both local and national publications—something I figured I could bring to the attention of a jury, if I was ever on the stand and needed to say: "You have the wrong guy. Look at this feature article on me in *Good Housekeeping* magazine. I build water features for a living. You want one?"

Who wouldn't want to live near a waterfall? Everyone likes being near water. It's the driving force of all nature. According to feng shui, water is considered a symbol of abundance, and if you live near it, preferably moving water, it's said to bring wealth and prosperity into your life. You don't think it's a coincidence that most people want to be near water when they book a vacation, do you? I don't, because I know our bodies subconsciously crave being near water. Probably because we're made up of about sixty percent water and we continuously gravitate toward what we are. After all, like attracts like.

"GOOD MORNING, Eric! My waterfall stopped running again," I heard Kendra, my pond customer, say through my phone. "Can you come over and fix it today? I'll be home alone all afternoon."

"Is the pump plugged in?" I asked, knowing the last time I did a service call for that problem she had simply unplugged the pump.

"Ummm . . . I'm not sure. I was really hoping you could come help me with it. Ethan's out of town all week," she replied, in a submissive tone. "You can charge me."

Ethan was Kendra's forty-five-year-old husband. He was a busy executive for a public company who spent a lot of time flying to meetings in a private Gulfstream III, while Kendra's main job was to get waxed, gelcoat her nails, highlight her hair, gloss her lips, and shop for outfits that revealed every curve she had perfected in her home gym. This was the bonus of my pond business: the eye candy of well-manicured housewives. I rarely saw the husbands around. I only dealt with them when we signed the contract and when they cut me checks for 20k at the end of the job. Other than that, the housewives had my number on speed dial, and Kendra called me the most, because she knew what she wanted—excitement.

As SOON AS I arrived in Kendra's backyard, like usual, I saw the plug removed from the electrical outlet. The waterfall was nestled up close to a large terraced deck, which overlooked an inground pool, with an attached hot tub. Next to that sat a modern pool house with an outdoor kitchen, which housed a full bar and a wood-fired pizza oven. The yard was immaculate. Luxury could be sensed in every detail. I just couldn't tell if the yard was built to be used, or out of fear of looking average.

While walking toward the electrical outlet attached to the house, I heard the sliding glass door open. I looked up, and there was Kendra, in a black silk robe. The robe was shorter than a valance and probably cost more than most people make in a week.

"Hi, Eric!" Kendra said, in her forty-year-old, sultry voice. She looked flawless leaning against the door, holding a chilled glass of white.

"Hi, Kendra," I replied, with my twenty-two-year-old smile.

"I'm not sure what's wrong with the waterfall," Kendra said, pointing her toes seductively.

I smiled again, playing stupid. "It looks like one of the landscaping guys unplugged it again."

"Ugh . . . I wish they'd pay attention to detail like you, Eric," Kendra replied, giving me a subtle stare. "Can I offer you some wine?"

"Thank you, but I have to run to another project. I'll plug the pump in, and I'll remove the string algae from the stream and waterfall."

"Bummer. . . . Well, if you change your mind, come get me. I'll be up in my bedroom reading," she said with a soft wink.

I couldn't do it. I couldn't go into Kendra's bedroom without Ethan's permission. I'd built a friendship with him. He taught me about big business. If I checked in on his pond on a Sunday, the one day he was home, he'd mentor me over cigars. Maybe he and Kendra had an open relationship, but I wasn't sure, and I respected him too much to cross that line. I thought about being in his shoes, working eighty-hour weeks, buying the wife whatever she wanted, then leaving her alone by the pool, looking for something to spike her day. What if I worked myself to death, while the pool guy held my wife? I didn't know. Maybe sharing is caring. Ethan did say, "Happy wife, happy life."

As I squatted down to pull the string algae out of the waterfall, I thought about all the couples I worked for. . . . I noticed that if one partner had more idle time than the other, the easier it was for them to slip in different directions. For example, if one partner had a goal, and the other was living aimlessly outside of that goal, I witnessed their discord. Conversely, the couples who were active toward the same goals seemed to be the closest. It appeared like they talked with each other more than they talked with their friends. They relaxed around their ponds and focused on constructive thought processes, ones that all had one thing in common—good communication.

I learned a lot from my mature pond customers. I learned that trust is formed by solid communication. I learned that solid communication happens when you talk about what you want, need, and feel—without the fear of being judged. I learned it's a place where you can be vulnerable. I also learned it's a place where you must be totally transparent with your partner. If she asks if you have another girlfriend, you can't say "no" and have a hooker you bang lines with on Tuesdays and Thursdays. Most importantly, important issues need to be discussed face-to-face, not over the phone or via text. Because texting can kill a relationship faster than a bullet on Adderall.

MY DOUBLE LIFE was in full swing, and the hardest part was figuring out which bridges to cross and which to burn, because in the underworld, bridges are burned regularly for mutual protection from government investigations.

"I smell weed. Were you smoking?" I asked Etu's Native American driver.

"Not me," he replied, stepping out of the truck. He was a kid, around my age, delivering a $200,000 load to one of my stash houses in Saratoga.

I had never exchanged more than a couple words with Etu's drivers, in case they had a wire on.

These handoffs were always tense, but I was even shorter than usual this time, because a month earlier parts of the World Trade Center had collapsed and prompted the setup of random police checkpoints within one hundred miles of the Canadian border. Now everyone was on high alert, because the odds of vehicles being profiled, pulled over, and searched for "terrorist activity" had heightened. It also made it a struggle for Etu's crew to smuggle weed into the United States to fill my ever-increasing orders. They had to ferry it in small batches over the Saint Lawrence River, in a tiny speedboat, with night-vision goggles on. Etu said he was frustrated with the tedious operation and recommended I find access to a commercial loading dock in Saratoga, with the promise he'd start shipping me larger loads, hidden amongst eighteen-wheeler lumber trucks coming from Canada. I dismissed his advice, though, intimidated by how a federal judge would perceive me if I was caught unloading weed off a semi-truck.

I probably made the wrong choice, because as soon as Etu's driver popped the hood at my stash house, a plume of smoke emerged from the engine compartment, forcing me to step back. I could now see where the burning weed smell was coming from —Etu had stuffed weed under the hood of his black Chevy after he couldn't fit it all in the hydraulic stash compartment located under the truck's bed. It was an unfortunate choice, because the heat from the truck's engine was now smoldering the plastic-wrapped weed.

"Holy fuck! You're lucky you didn't hit a roadblock," I said to the driver, as he stood silent in awe, probably counting his bless-ings. "Can I please use your sat phone to call Etu?" I asked, wanting a discount on the burned weed.

Etu's crew used satellite phones to communicate in the remote terrain of the Adirondacks.

"Sure, but he's not in a good mood. He was robbed for a half-million last night and had to flee a shoot-out."

The driver further explained that Etu had tried to sell my load to new customers, who were willing to pay more than me. But during the deal, at some desolate location on the reserva-tion, the crew pulled a gun on him.

Etu was able to escape unscathed on his four-wheeler, but he had to leave the weed behind as undercover agents rushed onto the scene. Supposedly the new crew had come up from New York City, but were unknowingly being followed by the DEA, which was secretly observing the deal in the distance and felt obligated to step in when a gun was pulled. Needless to say, that was the last order I ever took from Etu. As soon as I heard the letters "DEA," I knew I needed to walk away. And that's when I realized all relationships eventually come to an end, but with that end there always comes a new beginning—and I love new beginnings. They're when I let go of all my failures and disappointments. Actually, I crave new beginnings. They're when I reset and refocus.

11

IMPOTENT

I t was early morning in late summer of 2003, and I was finally in a steady groove with my new suppliers: some from the past and some whom I'd recently been introduced to through various acquaintances. Things remained stressful, but I accepted it, because I was paid handsomely for doing so. Plus, I knew how to alleviate stress by retreating to my inner stillness with the assistance of drugs, ones that provided me with temporary relief, but that also came with side effects—many of which were worse than my original problem.

I awoke to the sun piercing through my bedroom blinds, and a searing hangover. I was in a small double-wide on Saratoga Lake that I'd rented for the season. The last thing I had remembered was that two girls and myself were in my boat, in the middle of the glass lake under the moonlit sky, double-fisting Jose Cuervo bottles, while dancing to Biggie Smalls' "Ten Crack Commandments" blaring through the boat's speakers. But now I was lying in bed with over half a million in twenties stashed beneath it, and two beautiful women on top of it—one on each side of me—both passed out, face-down, wearing only their panties. I still had my swimsuit on, which made it a sure bet that I hadn't touched either of them that night.

Someone should've called Houston, because I had a problem. I was twenty-four, and my penis didn't work properly. Between the OxyContins I'd been snorting, my lack of exercise, and my daily grind, my erections could've made it on *America's Funniest Home Videos*. I doubt the Red Cross would've accepted my blood. My diet consisted of gas station food, and my weekends consisted of partying with enough drugs to easily put most people in a coma. I'd party until I blacked out. It was the only way I knew how to escape work, and these blackouts caused so many blockages in me that I could have easily been written off as a loss—even though I was finally a millionaire.

As I slowly got out of bed, I was careful not to wake the two girls. I was a little unsteady on my feet, but I made my way down the hallway and into the living room, where I could see: a half-eaten pizza, empty bottles of about six different kinds of booze, two rolled-up hundred-dollar bills, some flip-flops, and two bikini tops on the floor like little flags from Spring Break.

I poured myself a glass of water and sat down at the kitchen table while my eyes adjusted to the sunlight sparkling off the lake. As I leaned back in my chair, I stared into the reflection of my boat on the glassy water while contemplating my life choices. I couldn't believe it: I'd had my first organ failure on a night that should've been in my scrapbook. What an embarrassment—I had failed as a man.

Right then, my Motorola flip phone rang.

I got up, rummaged through the couch, and found it on the last ring before voicemail.

"Yo," I answered, in my thick, groggy voice.

"Did you hear?"

It took me a few seconds, but I realized it was Rob from college.

"Hear what?" I asked.

"Steve-O. He's gone."

"What?" I replied in disbelief.

"Yeah, he died . . . last night. His roommate found him cold on the couch this morning."

Right after college, before Rob moved to Utah for the best skiing conditions in the country, he'd introduced me to his childhood friend, Steve-O, a small-time drug dealer who became a regular customer of mine and whom I'd seen the night before for a quick deal.

I didn't know Steve-O outside of our dealings, but I did know I snorted some of his pills with him the previous night that probably did him in, and after I'd hung up with Rob, I said a brief prayer. I was going to miss Steve-O, but I definitely wasn't going to miss the pharmaceuticals he always gave me, which I always took, and had a major misconception about. I believed that since they were prescribed by doctors, they weren't danger-ous. But I can say, out of all the drugs I did, I've come to realize pharmaceuticals were the most taxing and the easiest to take. In turn, my habitual use of them slowly robbed me of my physical strength, like a steady bleed.

I wasn't addicted to pills, but I do know addiction can come from legitimate medications, prescribed by legitimate doctors, who are advised by ex-cheerleaders turned pharmaceutical reps. I also doubt the pharmaceutical industry is solely in the busi-ness of creating cures, because I know how drug dealers think. They're in the business of creating customers. It doesn't make financial sense for drug dealers to develop a completely non-addictive opiate. Drug dealers need to focus on bottom lines to stay in business, and they increase when customers return for *more*. It's business 101, but I can say, after all the pills I have tried, there isn't a chemical solution for spiritual problems.

·   ·   ·

I DON'T CRY MUCH, but I shed some tears at Steve-O's funeral. Watching his casket drop humbled me and reminded me that his nice car, expensive watch, girlfriend, and money weren't going with him. It was all gone, and *gone* was the word that changed me. I no longer needed to be "on" all the time to have a successful life. Partying exhausted me. It diminished the quality of my existence. Sure, I valued the human interaction at the beginning of the parties, but once I couldn't see straight, they were a waste of time—because all I really wanted to be doing was lounging with a good woman, and I now knew I wasn't going to find her being blitzed. I'd meet her when I was centered, but to get centered I needed to make some changes. So that's what I did, and I started by socializing differently. I'd still go out and party, but I was more selective and my meetings had an expiration time. It was after about two drinks.

I liked getting home early; it's where I recharged and recentered myself. It's also where I set my intentions—for one main purpose: to create more predictability in my unpredictable life.

A WEEK after Steve-O's funeral, I was in my home office preparing a proposal for a one-acre pond at a nearby estate. I had my laptop open on the desk in front of me, ready to access my Yahoo email, via the Yahoo homepage. Then, in the bottom right corner of the screen, a tiny clickable window popped up, with a beautiful girl's picture in it. "Hi, Eric! My name is Jill. I want to meet you," it said.

Yeah, right, I thought. But I looked again. The girl was sitting on a rock in a stream, with a waterfall behind her. It looked like one of the waterfalls I'd built, except it was real. Jill looked real, too. She looked like my dream girl: blonde, blue-eyed, and organic.

"Hi, Jill. Nice to meet you," I whispered to the screen.

Under Jill's photo, the ad said, "Yahoo Personals! Join for $19.99."

I had no idea what online dating was, but Jill was perfectly designed for me. Healthy, good symmetry, and in front of a waterfall for good measure. She seemed too good to be true. For a second, I wondered if she worked for the DEA. Maybe she was a cop, sent to infiltrate my organization. But with little hesitation I plugged in my credit card number, and within minutes I was henpecking away at the keyboard.

"Hi Jill:) Your pictures are beautiful. I like the waterfall, too. I have a small business building water features."

To my surprise, Jill wrote back the next day, and after a few email exchanges, I found out she was twenty-three years old and had recently quit her nanny gig in New York City to move to Woodstock, New York, for a more secluded life as a waitress at a farm-to-table restaurant. We wrote to each other every day for several weeks, and I'm embarrassed to say, I spent a lot of time telling her about the places I'd been, the things I'd accomplished, and the things I had. I was bragging. I was selling myself, hoping she'd stay engaged, because I liked reading her notes. I liked that there was always one waiting for me when I got home, and by the time our first date arrived, I was already in love. Not because I was lonely, but because I was ready—ready to "be there for each other."

I timed my first date with Jill after a half-million-dollar deal I had in Woodstock, so I wouldn't have to make the three-hour round trip twice.

When I pulled into the dirt driveway of Jill's rundown rental cabin, I parked and securely stashed my gym bag full of cash under the rear bench seat in the cab of my truck. As I walked to Jill's door, she opened it to greet me, and I stalled in my steps. I was surprised, but not pleasantly. She was missing the glow I'd seen in her pictures. I'd been catfished, but I didn't want to hurt her feelings, so I smiled at the same time she did.

Jill was about five-foot-six, 120 pounds, and had a black Celtic ring tattoo around her wrist, matching her thick black eyeliner. She didn't look as innocent and pure as I'd imagined, but I already loved the image that I'd created of her in my head, and Mom like always said, "Looks fade; personality lasts a lifetime." So I quickly looked through what I saw and continued walking toward Jill standing on the front step. And when she stooped down, she gave me a hug and a kiss on the cheek. The interaction felt real. I think it was our first form of showing that we mattered to each other.

Our date didn't involve going anywhere—it was set to be at her cabin—and when we stepped inside, I could tell the place probably dated back a couple generations. It smelled moldy. I could see various water stains on the ceiling from past roof leaks. The place felt hollow, too. There wasn't any furniture— just a scarf over a lampshade, a trippy canvas painting on the wall, and a couple of throw pillows on the wood floor—in front of a wood stove. It felt like a shack, and I liked it. I liked it because she was probably living within her means. I liked the hot glow of the fire, too. I could feel it radiating through the glass doors of the wood stove.

"Sorry, I don't have a couch. The pillows are only temporary," Jill said. "Please, make yourself comfortable."

"Don't be sorry. There's no better place to sit than near a fire," I replied, knowing coming home to a woman near a fire was part of my dream.

Jill set out a charcuterie board on the floor between me and the fire. It looked perfect, and as she popped open a bottle of Shiraz, I sensed she was ready for sex and that's when I became nervous.

I still didn't know if I could resemble all the things I'd seen in the movies. Between the images, music, dialogue, lighting, and special effects . . . sex was still intimidating. It seemed like a fantasy world, one I had to recreate perfectly to avoid rejection. Fuck, I'm embarrassed to say . . . Hollywood's money, power, and glamour made me feel weak and insecure in so many ways. It sure kept me busy, though. I wanted to be a hero like all the guys I'd seen in the movies. A hero to impress the right woman—one who would love me for everything I thought I was supposed to be.

"So tell me, Mr. Canori, what's your story?" Jill asked, settling beside me on the floor.

"That's a big question," I replied, gazing into the fire's flame. "I suppose I'm just trying to make a living. The only problem is, I haven't had time to live. I'm always working."

Jill nodded, looking deeper into the flame with me. "Tell me more," she said.

"Are my secrets safe with you?" I asked.

"I won't even put them in my diary."

We both laughed, and as Jill inched closer, I felt my insides relax.

"I sell weed on the side. I started when I was younger—mostly to escape from my family."

Jill wasn't even surprised. I could tell she had a story, too, but she didn't know how much weed I sold or that she was the first person I was opening up to.

"I also had a difficult childhood. But I've learned you can't escape from your family. The only thing you can really do is change our response to them," Jill said.

I reflected for a moment, sensing Jill's intellect. She was smart, and I started feeling safe with her and she started feeling safe with me. Not enough to have sex, though. Instead, we ended up cuddling by the fire, and opening our hearts more. Our date was about honesty and vulnerability, two topics of discussion that solidified I was in love before the night was over. She told me about her childhood struggles, and I told her about mine and my dream, admitting I wanted to make it a reality with her.

Jill was one-third city, one-third goth, and one-third hippie. Which in my mind, added up to lost but well-traveled. And if I hadn't been street smart, it would've been tough for me to read into her deep stare, which I came to realize wasn't her grilling me. It was just her way of trying to figure out why everything she wanted in life was a moving target—one I wanted to help her hit, so she'd be there for me when I came home from work each night. There were only so many years I could drive 50,000 miles alone, just to come home and be alone too.

WITHIN LESS THAN A MONTH, I led with my money and moved Jill into my house in Saratoga. We did what other young couples do: shop for groceries, watch movies, travel to warm beaches, talk about the future, and hit nitrous oxide tanks on the holidays. Yeah, Jill could party if the occasion arose, and she was completely on board with my weed business. She even packed me healthy meals when I needed to drive a shipment of grass to St. Louis, or the Carolinas for a quick 30k profit. I think it turned her on when I outbid Mariah Carey on a small yacht charter, or outran a speeding ticket in a Porsche. I also think she felt safe when all our bills were paid on time. But soon things started to fall apart. It was the point in a relationship where I usually find out who I am. The point where I'm either part of the problem or part of the solution.

One year in, Jill wanted a ring, but something in me couldn't say "I do," and when I couldn't, Jill's unmet expectations put pressure on me. I felt if I didn't propose to her I'd have to face negative consequences. I didn't like that feeling, and I couldn't understand why she required so much, so fast. It seemed there was always some new piece of furniture, jewelry, or knickknack that would complete her, and now it was a ring.

I started thinking maybe her wants stemmed from the unrealistic standards set by Barbie and Ken. I'd wished she had understood how advertisers try to define "love" so that they can extract money from our pockets. It's Marketing 101, and it had us running in circles. I just wanted to fall asleep with Jill, wake up, go to work, and do it all over again the next day. Why did we need a Lexus to remember December? Did we really need a white picket fence to feel safe? Someone would've had to repaint the slats every few years anyway.

Fuck, I wasn't smuggling weed internationally to hire a painter for some material eyesore. I worked so we could take time off to spend more time together. Isn't that what it's all about? *Free time* to enjoy each other? If we kept spending more money on more things, I'd die on the job before we could be thankful for all that we already had. I sometimes wondered if Jill wanted me or my money. Either one was fine, I just wanted the honest truth, because I could get a reliable escort in any major city, any night of the week.

The truth is, I wasn't home much, and when I was, Jill told me, "All you're good for is your endless wallet," and she was right. I was sluggish in bed and I unknowingly was using my money to hold us together. My overall take on the relationship was—we made it. I assumed since we met each other, I could check her off my list as "done," and all we had to do was exist. Meanwhile, her list still had things on it like: Marriage, House, Friends, and Family. The problem was, her list wasn't my priority, and when Jill blamed me for letting her down, I blamed her for expecting too much. And soon we were arguing every week, constantly threatening to break up. She often said she was going to leave if I didn't change, but I didn't listen. However, I listened very closely the last time we spoke over the phone, while I was driving home with $400,000 after delivering a load to Boston.

"Hi, Beautiful, what's for dinner?" I asked.

"There's no dinner tonight. I moved my stuff out and I'm not coming back."

I felt my chest drop. "Why? Can we at least have one last meal?"

"I'm leaving for good this time. There is no future between us. Please don't call me again or try to convince me otherwise."

I heard the click of the disconnected call.

Jill was right, there was no future. I was too scared to commit. Partially because Kendra's husband's advice often echoed in my head: "Eric, the number one cause of divorce is marriage."

WHEN I ARRIVED home from Boston that night, I walked into the house and found that Jill really was gone. As I stood alone in our kitchen, holding my duffel bag of cash, I looked around, and the house felt empty. Jill had removed all of her furniture, her knick-knacks, and even her silverware. She had pulled a Houdini, and my heart sank in denial because I knew she was definitely gone this time.

My fingers were shaky as I dialed Jill, but it went straight to voicemail. "Come home, please," I said after the beep.

After I ended the message, I stared at the phone in my hand, hoping it would ring, but it didn't. So I went into the bedroom and rolled into bed, hoping sleep would put an end to the night and she'd call back in the morning. But the minute I hit the pillow, I became even more awake. All the *whys*, *ifs*, and *hows* started running through my mind. I tossed and turned, hoping a different position might help, but no, I just spent most of the night checking the alarm clock, with an unfamiliar pain in my chest. I think it was the first night I ever realized I had a heart. It hurt, and it hurt even more when I pretended it didn't hurt. I wanted Jill in my arms more than ever. I loved her. I confided in her. *How could she do this?* I thought. Slowly, my heartache turned to frustration, and by 4 a.m. I realized sleep was out of the question and that I needed the next sweetest thing in my life ... the fruit of my hard labor.

I wandered into the kitchen and grabbed the duffel bag of cash on the floor. I then went down into the basement and grabbed another couple duffel bags of cash I had stashed between the floor joists. I grabbed my money counter, too, and headed into the garage. I dropped all the cash on a couple fold-out tables and plugged the counter in. I wrapped a T-shirt around my face so I wouldn't breathe in the filth that came off the bills as they ran through the machine. I then reached for the shelf that my stereo was sitting on and popped in a Rolling Stones CD. I pressed "play" and turned the volume to "max." "Beast of Burden" started playing loud, as I began feeding stacks of cash into the counter.

Not knowing where Jill had moved to, or if I'd ever see her again, was now turning my frustration to anger. All I could do was hope my familiar cash counting routine would hypnotize me, as it always had. But it didn't, not even after I'd neatly stacked over $2 million. That's when I started to bargain with myself, saying that I'd give away all my money if Jill came back home.

NOTHING COULD VAPORIZE the heartache I experienced over the next several weeks. I was twenty-six years old, worth close to $5 million, and heartbroken. I wanted to talk about it with some-one, but all I did was whisper "I'm fine" to myself. And it was an awkward moment when I realized I wasn't as important as I'd thought. I'd always just assumed if I paid the bills, Jill would stay with me. But it seemed she needed more. Sure, we took vacations, took pictures of the vacations, put the pictures in the vacation album, then went back to work, made more money, and saved up for a better vacation and a fancier photo. But as I looked at all our old vacation photos, they became less real to me.

I remembered an argument we'd had only hours before each one was taken. All it would take was for me to smile at our waitress the "wrong way," and our night would be ruined. Our arguments weren't healthy either. They were "I'm right and you're wrong." And Jill always had the last word in any argument, and anything that I'd say after that began a new argument. I wasn't a saint either. Many times after an argument, I'd spend time thinking about clever things I could've said, rather than reflecting on what she'd said. I didn't listen. I focused on victory —not progress. And when she eventually said, "Whatever," I just figured I'd won. In hindsight, I think listening, processing, and discussing a win-win may have kept us together for another year, but in the end, our values were too different. She wanted to settle down, and I was just gearing up. Plus, it would have been foolish to settle down with someone who couldn't give me a clear picture of what they wanted in life . . . unless I wanted to run in circles to my casket.

I never saw Jill again to apologize properly, and I didn't chase her—I replaced her. I hired a private chef and a masseuse to come to the house three times per week. I bought a new truck, a new wardrobe, and several parcels of vacant land. The only thing I hadn't bought yet was sex, because even though I had accepted Jill was gone, it took me several months to work through the hole in my heart.

Letting go of Jill was hard. I wanted to explain my behavior to her. I wanted her to understand my past. I wanted her to understand the daily risks and sacrifices I'd made to provide for us. But eventually I recognized her opinions wouldn't pay the bills, so I stopped caring, and accepted she didn't know who I was. Actually, I didn't know who I was either. Although I did know I wasn't the soft lover I'd tried to be. Fuck, I was an outlaw with buried pain and something to prove. The only problem was, I didn't know what I had to prove, who my audience was, or where the finish line was.

12

HEARTACHE, CASH, AND ESCORTS

A
ll I could see were concrete buildings, steel shipping containers, and wooden pallets among a large area of blacktop riddled with potholes. I was at a rundown warehouse in New Jersey, on a freezing February night, and I'd just finished unloading over a million dollars worth of weed secreted in an eighteen-wheeler, stuffed with furniture, from British Columbia. I noticed additional weed in the back of the tractor-trailer, but I didn't ask any questions. It was a new supplier, and I was just testing out their product and service, because with Jill gone, I could now take bigger risks because I had less to lose, and no one to be responsible for—except myself. Even so, being in a quiet commercial warehouse district, at midnight, with out-of-state plates, was a sloppy risk. The deal was supposed to go down at 7 p.m., but I was told there was a holdup at the border. I didn't complain, though, because I was now willing to do whatever it took to make millions. It was an attitude that was impossible to stop.

By midnight, my GMC Sierra was stuffed to the gills with top-shelf weed. I had 250 pounds in the covered bed and another 100 pounds in the extended cab, behind my heated leather seats.

Before I pulled away from the loading dock, I popped on my dome light and took another quick look at the printed Mapquest directions to my newly vetted customer in Brooklyn. I then reached for one of my burner phones in my center console and texted the new customer: "ETA 12:45am."

For safety, I always kept all my underground contacts on prepaid burner phones, so nothing was attached to anyone's real name. My only legitimate phone was the one for my water feature customers. Other than that, all the others were dead-end leads.

As I headed toward the George Washington Bridge, the roads were empty and I felt noticeable, so I turned on some Pink Floyd to calm me. New York City was intimidating as I approached, but I knew how to drive around the city because Jim had taught me years ago, when he and Mom once drove me there with a packed family cooler to look at the Statue of Liberty. I remember Jim saying, "If you don't drive fast, you'll get run over," as he blew by yellow cabs in our Ford Explorer, with his feet rapidly switching between clutch, gas, and brake. My head would bobble around in the back seat as I noticed all the different colors of people, carrying all different bags of *stuff*. I wondered why everyone was in such a rush, and Mom commented, "Life moves fast, Eric. Enjoy the little things, because one day you'll look back and realize they were big things." I had no idea what she meant; I only knew I wanted to do big things.

As I approached the Triborough Bridge leading into Brooklyn, alarms went off in my head to the sight of several officers standing around the toll booths. *What are they doing here?* I thought. Is this a normal occurrence? I didn't know; I was a small-town kid.

Before I pulled up to the tollbooth, I relaxed my face and straightened my checked Oxford in the mirror. This was exactly why I dressed like I'd just stepped out of a J.Crew dressing room, so I wouldn't get profiled as a drug dealer. Jill often said I needed a hipper look, but I liked blending in and being thought of as an innocent kid who worked with computers. It allowed me to slip through the cracks for years. I must say, though, my outfits were definitely out of the norm for my industry, considering the guy I'd just met wore a turban, and the guy before that had a wallet chain and rode a Harley. I think my suppliers took me as a joke upon first sight, but once they witnessed my flow, they knew I was a power player because I never had excuses—only results.

As I rolled down my window at the tollbooth, I saw a vehicle pulled over ahead and the driver being questioned.

Thoughts began bouncing between my ears. Are they allowed to search vehicles? If I get busted now, will Jill come help me?

Before I knew it, the toll officer made eye contact with me, and quickly took a glimpse at the inside of my truck. All I could see was his silver badge; his blue uniform was just a blur. I'm not even sure what type of badge it was or what it said, but it definitely made my heart skip a few beats . . . and after he took my cash, he didn't say a word, so I coasted off slowly.

I couldn't fucking believe it; I made it through the toll without one question asked. I assumed the officers must have been tired, because there weren't many other vehicles around to occupy their attention, except mine.

I accelerated more, then more, then slapped my dashboard a couple times, shouting, "Big Rig, you did me right again!" Yeah, I secretly named my truck "Big Rig," because I did over fifty thousand miles per year on her at night, when only the big trucks were on the road and everyone else was sleeping. She was my girl. She protected me, and I bought the same fully loaded GMC

Sierra, new, every year. Even in the same color, so no one could tell it was new and start asking questions. Ones that could have led from "How did you afford that?" to "How did you get third-row seats in front of Naomi Campbell to Jay-Z's coming out of retirement concert?" to "Why are there over a dozen prepaid burner phones in your center console?"

Fortunately, I never had to answer any of those questions, but I knew there was one answer for all of them, and that is: When you're a drug dealer, you always get what you want. The only catch is, it can all get taken away in a second.

Once I hit the quiet side streets of Brooklyn, I kept one eye on the rearview and one on the street signs. It was new territory, so I remained cautious as I continued following my turn-by-turn Mapquest directions through an endless maze of dark, barren streets, lined with looming warehouses, until I finally found the garage I was looking for. It was off Lorimer Street, in Greenpoint. And when I arrived, I picked up my burner and texted "here."

In less than ten seconds, there was a knock on my window and I jumped a little at the sight of a tall, bald dude peering inside my truck.

"You're late," he said, as my power window retracted.

"Good things take time," I replied, scanning the perimeter for any suspicious activity or unmarked cars.

"Streets" was his nickname, and I was a little jumpy because I'd heard rave reviews about his business ethics. I only hoped I could meet his standards, because he was a cash-on-delivery customer and could take endless amounts of weed, if the price and quality matched.

"Pull in," he said, stepping back away from my truck.

I backed into the garage, which was just a ten-by-thirty-foot concrete room. Streets then lowered and locked the aluminum garage door in front of me, as I stepped out of my truck.

When we shared a firm handshake, I introduced myself as

"Jack," and within a minute I pulled out eight large duffel bags from my truck and laid them on the dusty, cracked concrete floor. Streets then zipped open one of the duffle bags and pulled out a pound.

I felt proud when Streets sliced into the plastic, took a whiff, and rolled the bag around in his hand, studying it.

"Looks all right," he said, clearly not impressed, or pretending not to be. I wasn't sure which, but I happened to know it was some of the best bulk indoor weed anywhere on the East Coast and I wanted to call bullshit, but I kept my mouth shut, because it was his show and I didn't want to say anything that could potentially sour the deal.

Streets was a potential gold mine. New York City was in general, but it was also the most competitive wholesale weed market in the United States, and if my numbers didn't add up there, I wouldn't be remembered—I'd be forgotten.

Streets knew my weed was priced right, though, because seconds later, he hoisted a laundry bag of cash out of a large steel jobsite toolbox, bolted to the floor, in the back corner of the garage.

As Streets dragged the bag toward me, I grabbed it from him and lifted it onto the open tailgate of my truck. It felt like it weighed close to one hundred pounds, and when I peeked inside, I could see the rubber-banded bundles of cash, which I didn't bother to count, because by this time in the game, if I knew the denominations of the bills, I could easily estimate how much money there was by the weight of the bag.

Bills weigh about 1 gram each, and this bag definitely felt like $1.2 million. I also knew I only stood to make about three percent on the deal, but profit wasn't my priority at the moment . . . networking and expansion was.

"You have a nice spot here," I said, standing next to my truck, impressed by the discreet location, in the middle of a busy city.

"Yeah, but it'll probably be the last time you use it," he replied, adjusting his eyes on mine. "If you prove to be reliable, I'm going to get a separate garage, exclusively for you, and give you the key. You'll be able to drop as much work as you want there."

Streets had no clue who I was, or that I was also vetting him, because my life was still revealed on a need-to-know basis. No one needed to know I was on track to do over $50 million in sales that year, and in my eyes Streets had to prove his value if he wanted to stay in my unknown circle. But I didn't tell him that, because my entire business depended on discretion, even though I secretly craved that "pat on the back."

I sometimes wished I could have been recognized for my accomplishments, but I couldn't in this industry. They needed to remain private, which meant my profession was lonely at times and I had to learn how to make good friends with myself. That was a challenge, though, because in the process I had to face myself, which was probably my most difficult chore in life. I think it is for most people. It's not work, friendships, or family. No, it's having to deal with ourselves every single day, which many of us don't have time for. Mainly because we're too busy dealing with other people's moods, or finding things to keep ourselves busy. At least that's how it was for me. I was really good at keeping myself busy.

It was 1 a.m. when I hopped in my truck and left Streets, and after I had made it a couple blocks away from him, I silently congratulated myself for finishing another day outside of handcuffs, before pushing the blue button on my rearview mirror.

"Hello Mr. Canori, this is Cynthia with OnStar. How may I be of assistance?" I heard through the Bose speakers of my truck.

"Hi, Cynthia, can you please help me find a plush five-star hotel room in Manhattan for tonight please?"

"I'd be happy to assist, Mr. Canori. Please allow me one moment."

I pulled over to the side of the street and waited, while reaching into my console for Jay-Z's first album, *Reasonable Doubt*.

"Hi, Mr. Canori, I found availability at the beautiful Pierre Hotel this evening. It's located on East 61st Street. Would you like me to reserve you a room and route you directions?"

"Please do, Cynthia!"

I only used OnStar directions for personal use and the pond business, never for locations to weed deals. I actually wished my OnStar was disconnected altogether, to avoid potential government tracking. In fact, I did ask the car dealership to disconnect it, but they told me it couldn't be removed from the vehicle. They said it was an electronic security feature that would disable the vehicle when tampered with. But I took other precautions to avoid being tracked, such as removing the batteries out of my personal Palm Trio and all my burners, when doing deals, to avoid being pinged by the government.

Once OnStar routed the hotel directions to me, I slid *Reasonable Doubt* into the deck and maxed out the volume. Soon after, a crisp baseline thumped through my speakers, accompanied by Jay-Z's lyrics: *"Chilly with enough bail money to free a big willie."*

I started bobbing my head to the beat. I felt alive! New York City wasn't just a place; it was a feeling. Its sparkling lights perked me up while Jay-Z's lyrics simultaneously struck chords deep within me, as I rapped along, *"My life is based on sacrifices. Holdin' more drugs than a pharmacy . . ."*

Jay-Z's flow inspired me and his loud music distracted me into happiness. Actually, it distracted me from having to face myself. I think that's why I rarely drove alone in silence. I didn't want to hear my own thoughts. Subconsciously, I assumed dwelling on my mistakes, shortcomings, and personal problems was a waste of time. Only when I neared my destination would I turn down the volume, so I could focus on parking. Otherwise, I played my music loud enough to overload my brain, the same way drugs had. This is how I escaped my reality. The only problem was—I could never find my way back.

"Hello, you must be Mr. Canori," greeted the young girl working the night shift at the front desk of the Pierre Hotel.

"That's me," I replied, with a smile, as she smiled back.

The opulent lobby was trafficless at 1:30 a.m. on a weeknight, and I felt awkward holding a heavy laundry bag of cash, without any other luggage. I felt she could see through the bag, or possibly, even through me.

"I see you will be staying with us for just one night, Mr. Canori. Is that correct?"

"That's correct."

"And how would you like to pay for your room, Mr. Canori?"

"Cash, please."

I was starting to like the sound of Mr. Canori. Streets called me "Jack;" the guy before that had called me "Tom," another one of my aliases; and Jill called me "Asshole." But when I opened my wallet, I was "Mr. Canori," and I felt important. I felt like I'd finally proven myself, something I'd been trying to do all my life —probably because I was taught the more good I did, the more I'd be loved.

I think love was a conditional concept in my childhood. I never experienced unconditional love, at least that I'm aware of. The only thing I knew was that there were steps to being loved. First, I had to accomplish something. Then once I accomplished something, I'd get praised. And once I was praised, that's when I was accepted, or I suppose you could say: loved.

MY SUITE HAD A CITY VIEW, a king bed with crisp white sheets, and enough pillows to host a bachelorette party. But I only wanted one girl that night, and at that hour she could only be found in the thick yellow book sitting in the nightstand drawer. So I reached for the phone book and quickly flipped to the "Escorts" section—hoping an escort could take the edge off life, with no commitment on my part, because I knew slipping back into a loving relationship would've required effective communication and making compromises—two things I didn't have time for anymore.

I started tracing over every ad with my index finger. I saw the words "Secret pleasures, Fetish, Hottest, Role Playing, All Occasions, Dominatrix, Outcall," and then I saw an ad with the words: "European, Elite, Luxury, Finest, Discreet, and High-class." And that's what I wanted, VIP status, no matter the price.

As I dialed the number from the hotel room, my hands were shaky, because I was about to break another law, when I'd always told myself I'd only break one: drug trafficking.

"Pure Models, how can I help you?" a sexy voice answered.

"Hi, do you have any women available at this hour?"

"Sweetie, I have gorgeous Mia available for outcall right now. She's a dirty blonde, Ukrainian, 5'9", D-cup, size 36-26-36. You won't regret her. She's by-the-hour, very accommodating, and can stay as long as you'd like. It's two thousand for the first hour, and fifteen hundred for each additional hour."

"She sounds beautiful. Can we start with just one hour, please? Then go from there?"

While waiting for Mia with excitement and nervousness, I had room service delivered from the late-night menu. It was the first linen-covered table on wheels that I'd received since I was in Anguilla with Jill, and its arrival pushed a feeling of loneliness through me. It was always those little moments I remembered. The enjoyable ones. I forgot all the dull moments—not by choice, but by default.

I HEARD a knock on the door, then quickly finished my chicken liver paté, while tying my white terrycloth robe.

Sweet Louise! Mia was a fucking dime! She was a little different than described, but she definitely should've been on the cover of my yearbook. She was the kind of woman you'd see at a banquet on James Bond's arm, or in the Pierre Hotel elevator at 2 a.m. She was vibrant. She had a long, narrow face, straight, thin nose, dark eyes, and a clear complexion. I'd say she was about thirty-two years old. Her heels were pointy, her purse was made of crocodile, and her breasts were the first thing through the door.

"You're handsome!" Mia whispered quietly, not to wake the neighbors as she brushed past me, while I closed the door behind her.

"Thank you. You're beautiful," I whispered back. "May I take your coat?"

Mia spun around, looked into my eyes, caressed my cheek with one long red fingernail, and slowly ran her hand down my exposed chest, all in one fluid motion, and replied: "Please do."

As I reached for Mia's coat, she noticed the exposed hundreds in my robe pocket, and placed her hand on them and asked, "Is this mine?"

"Yeah, to start," I replied, with a smile.

"I love a good start, sweetie. May I use your bathroom to freshen up?"

I nodded my head, as Mia took the cash and slinked into the

white marbled bathroom. I could hear the *click clack* of her black stilettos on the floor behind the closed door, and after I moved the food cart into the doorway, I dimmed the lights and turned the heat up to 78. I figured the warm temperature would loosen me up, since I wasn't a drinker anymore.

When Mia emerged, my jaw dropped and my balls tightened. The goddess looked like she'd walked straight out of an Agent Provocateur photo shoot. The only thing she had on was a mesh bra and embroidered sheer panties. I was star-struck as she gently sat on the edge of the bed, crossing her legs, leaning into me, waiting for me to give her instructions.

"You're cute," she said, reaching over and running her nails up my leg.

My body twitched. I felt awkward, but I quickly reminded myself I was paying her to accept me for who I was.

"Thank you, you're beautiful," I replied, searching for the next respectful move.

Indeed, I wanted to fuck right then, but I didn't know how to initiate and I wasn't the type of guy to say, "Come over here and put those pretty lips on my cock."

"Is this your first time calling for a girl?" she asked, pulling her hair behind her shoulders.

"Yeah, my girl recently left me."

"Poor baby. Why did she leave?"

"I put work before her."

"I bet you did," she said, her hand now on my chest, making a lazy circle as her body inched closer to mine.

"Yeah, I fucked up," I replied, cheerlessly.

Mia stopped, resting her hand on the skin of my waist, and turned to look me in the eye as she said, "Honey, don't be so hard on yourself. Every guy I see puts work first. Their wives have expensive tastes that need to be funded," she giggled.

I was curious who her typical client was, so I asked, "What

type of clients do you have?"

"Oh, I have Wall Street guys, businessmen, even a few politicians. Mostly very wealthy men that don't want to get caught cheating with their co-workers. Some have their own jets and some have multiple homes, which they never use. Most have more money than they can keep track of."

"Are they happy?" I asked.

"Not really. That's why they call me," she said, smiling. "Last week, a client flew me to his Aspen house and he was too tired to even ski. He was young, too."

"Why are they unhappy?"

"They're tired of trying to keep up. They only stay with their wives for the kids' sake, and so they don't have to pay alimony. They don't have time to work out, and many are too tired for sex. Some clients just see me to talk."

I relaxed deeper into the soft bed, now lying on my back, with Mia lying to the left of me. I liked having her curled beside me, with her lips near my ears, and her breasts tight against my torso. But I wasn't solely focused on her breasts. I was also wondering if I was on track to become one of the unhappy guys she was describing—a guy who didn't have time to enjoy life.

Mia didn't know it, but she was helping me clarify who I was and what I wanted out of life, which was a woman who didn't need me to be happy. I wanted a woman who was secure on her own. A woman who didn't need me to make her feel whole. Fuck, I didn't have the energy to take on another project. Sure, initially I thought I could make Jill happy, but I was wrong, because I didn't even know how to keep myself happy.

I spent the next two hours unloading my heart to Mia about Jill and my childhood. It seemed being naked in bed with Mia was the healthiest way for me to talk—probably because I knew I'd never see her again, and the possibility of rejection was zero.

I actually talked deeper with Mia than I had with Jill. I never told Jill all the childhood trauma I was carrying around with me, and at times, I felt like I was living with a secret—one that I had to keep, because I felt like no one would like me if they knew everything about me.

I was embarrassed of my childhood, because I had missed out on years of socialization. I seriously spent the majority of my upbringing grounded—literally twiddling my thumbs and doodling in the margins of my spiral-bound notebooks—hoping for an adulthood lined with freedom. My bedroom didn't have a TV either, so when I wasn't doodling, I spent my days learning about life through the classic rock cassette tapes I listened to, while watching rain puddles form outside my bedroom window. And if it wasn't raining, I'd watch the squirrels collect food and chase each other. It's fair to say I spent so much time alone that I began to feel unworthy, and I think that unworthiness followed me into my adulthood and pushed me to isolate myself behind a career that allowed me to become so busy that I didn't have time to talk about my true feelings with anyone. I only had time to work or black out, while a hollow feeling remained below the surface.

But here I was now, an adult, and I was grateful for Mia's therapy session. It took until 5 a.m., and cost me $3,500, but it was well worth it. Mia told me to accept my losses and to work on myself. She said to view them as gifts that were putting me on the correct path. She said that before I formed another relationship I had to be happy with my own life first—otherwise my unhappiness would resurface in the new relationship and destroy it from the inside out, like cancer. She also said the sooner I found peace within myself, the sooner I'd be free. So that was the night I set myself free, with my confidence at an all-time high. It was Mia's words that propelled me to do so: "Eric, focus on what you can control, and forget what other people think about you."

13

THE FILM INDUSTRY

Over the next six months, my weed business took off. I developed accounts in every state on the East Coast between New Orleans and Boston. I had four trusted drivers who handled my out-of-state deliveries, and I also had four stash houses in Saratoga Springs, New York: one for receiving orders, one for packaging orders, one for inventory, and one for counting and storing money. I managed the entire operation with about fifteen burners I kept in a messenger bag nearby me at all times. I had a routine of powering on each phone at least once a day to check and see if I had new messages from customers, drivers, employees, or suppliers. I felt like an air traffic controller, but I still remained hands-on and did weekly short-distance deliveries to New York City. Remaining hands-on allowed me to keep a pulse on my organization in order to prevent any infiltration from the DEA.

When I was in New York City, I became a regular at the Four Seasons, Ritz, and Mandarin Oriental. I craved white glove service and the finest women that money could buy, from all parts of the globe. Every escort I saw had a different, unexpected purpose. Some scratched my back while I watched a movie, some fulfilled my bottled-up fantasies, and some helped me shed insecurities. And when I needed company on the nights I was stuck in Saratoga awaiting late-night border deliveries, I'd send a black car to pick up an escort in Manhattan and drive her three hours north to me.

The more escorts I saw, the more confident I became around them. Many of them taught me life lessons and healed me in countless ways. Eventually, I started hearing a common comment among them: "You're really good at getting me to open up, Eric. You'd make a good interviewer; you should have your own TV show."

After hearing that several times, I started thinking . . . maybe I could have my own TV show. Maybe I could show men and women around the world everything I was learning. Besides, I was getting bored of the weed game, and a TV show seemed to be a good avenue to replace the current income I was accustomed to. Plus, I'd been underground for so long that my ego had a desire to be seen. And my desire to be "seen" is all it took for me to sell my pond business and jump into the film industry with a four-man makeshift production crew.

The plan was for the crew to film me interviewing hundreds of women from across the country, with the intention of revealing the hidden truths behind a successful, modern relationship. My questions would revolve around how time, money, and sex played roles within the women's lives. I'd disseminate my findings via a web series that could hopefully help men and women avoid and cope with the difficulties in today's fast-paced relationships. The goal was to inspire people. Maybe even someone would look me in the eye and say, "Eric, because of you, I didn't give up," or maybe the show would only teach me. Either way, I wanted to be recognized for making an impact in the world.

Being recognized promoted a sense of belonging in my life. I think that's part of the reason why my business grew so fast. It was my desire to be seen and heard by others, because my value was tied to what other people thought about me. The problem was, that mindset was beginning to trap me. I was becoming a people pleaser. I do have an excuse, though; the quest for wholeness had never been taught to me.

It was summer, 2006, and I was at Camp Bisco, a multi-day music festival. I had received clearance from the festival's promoter to film my show on their premises. They gave me a prime spot, not far from the main stage, to park an RV I'd rented. They also gave my film crew access to a golf cart, with which to cruise the festival grounds and selectively gather women who wanted to be brought back to the RV and interviewed. The event was practice for us, to see how well we worked together, before we started taking the production more seriously.

I spared no expense in getting the footage I wanted. I had a small plane swoop me down 150 feet over the festival, with its door open, to collect B-roll footage, before descending me to the ground to interview a dozen women at the RV. The interviews went fast, because half the people who walked past our RV were tripping their face off, and I couldn't wait to be right there with them.

By the second night, I finished my interviews and ingested enough psychedelic mushrooms to meet my new and unexpected girlfriend. I first noticed her out of the corner of my eye, dancing to some electronic tribal music with trails of stage lights spinning through the otherwise dark crowd. I'm not sure when she noticed my dance moves, but she slowly circled toward me and we started stepping and turning at the same frequency. She was a brunette, five-foot-eight about 120 pounds, with a body tighter than a drum.

When the girl eventually brushed up against me, we melded our dances into one—with our bodies flowing in the same directions, at the same time. I'm sure to some our primal dance may have looked like a seizure, but to me, it felt like synchronicity.

Our dance eventually dissipated around 1 a.m., which led us into an intimate night that started with a kiss, revolved around a transcendent blow job, and finished with a cuddle. We didn't exchange one word the entire night, not on the concert field or in the bed of my RV. However, she did leave her number on my pillow, without a name, and it only took me one day to dial it. And before I knew it, I was two months into a committed relationship with Sarah, whom I soon privately named Trainwreck.

"ERIC, WHERE ARE YOU?" Sarah shouted, frantically. "You said you'd be here three hours ago! Hurry! I'm in pain, and they're out of rooms here."

Sarah was calling me from the lobby of the Hotel on Rivington, in the Lower East Side of Manhattan, where I'd thrown a penthouse promotional party the night before for my film production, now named *A Woman's Mind*.

"I'm running later than expected," I replied.

I was in Brooklyn picking up some cash owed to me, and still waiting on one more customer. Streets had just paid me, my Philly customer paid me the hour before, but my North Carolina customer was stuck in Jersey traffic and running late. So I prepared my calm voice, hoping Sarah would calibrate her tone to mine, because I'd recently seen the amount of pills prescribed to her for anxiety issues and had already witnessed a few of her outbursts around my film crew.

"What's wrong? You didn't take the pills yet, did you?" I asked.

"I took the first one," Sarah replied.

"Fuck—" I said, but quickly calmed myself before continuing on with: "I thought we agreed you'd wait until we got home to take them?"

"If I wanted to be controlled, I would've come with a remote!" she snapped back.

I'd mistakenly gotten Sarah pregnant within the first month of knowing her, although in my defense, she misled me into believing she was taking contraceptive pills. But now that her cycle was two weeks late, and after some strategic convincing from me, she was in possession of two pills to abort, which I'm not proud to admit, but is hopefully forgivable.

When I first met Sarah, she worked as a bookkeeper for a company in NYC, and unbeknownst to me, had a boyfriend in Florida that she'd visit on the weekends. But that all changed when she decided to maneuver her way into my lavish lifestyle by taking sick days from work to visit me more often, and, soon after, claiming that she'd lost her job and practically mandating that I give her one in my film production—in order to maintain her previous income. I felt forced to comply, too, in fear that she'd expose my illicit lifestyle to authorities if I didn't.

Unfortunately, I had to clue Sarah in on my operation, because it was near impossible for me to hide all my burner phones from her.

AROUND 10 P.M., I pulled up to the curbside of Hotel Rivington to meet Sarah. I live-parked my truck, stepped out of it, and walked around to the sidewalk to assist her. She was acting erratically as I quickly placed her suitcase in the truck, hoping she wouldn't draw much attention, since I had around $2.2 million in the truck's rear cab.

After I buckled Sarah into the front passenger seat, I checked my mirrors and nonchalantly coasted off.

"You need to find us a room, now!" Sarah demanded, raising her voice.

"We have to drive to Saratoga now. I have an important meeting there early in the morning," I replied firmly, knowing that I had two deliveries coming in from Canada the following day.

"All you care about is business! When are you going to fucking realize that you have a girlfriend?"

"When you calm the fuck down," I replied, keeping my eyes on all my mirrors.

"Find us a room now, or you'll regret it."

And that's all Sarah had to say for me to drive straight to the Mandarin Oriental in Columbus Circle, because if I didn't follow her orders, there was a good chance she'd have law enforcement searching my vehicle any minute.

WHEN WE PULLED up to the hotel, the bellman greeted us with his familiar wide smile, knowing my tips were always hundred-dollar bills. "Welcome back, Mr. Canori. Can I help you with your luggage?"

"Thank you, Randy, but I have fragile hard drives full of film footage. I'd prefer to handle them myself, if you don't mind."

Randy obliged, and I carefully placed two duffel bags and a suitcase on his baggage cart. All told, it was about two hundred pounds of cash.

I always felt like a king when I stayed at the Mandarin Oriental. It was my go-to spot. The spa there recharged me. It was the best of the best. I knew so, because Jay-Z was renting a penthouse there.

As Randy escorted us with his bellman cart at my side to guest services for check-in, Sarah kept looking at me as if I had no idea what I was doing in life. But what she didn't know is that

I already knew my path was different. I wasn't lost on it, either—at least not yet.

After checking in, Randy allowed me to privately take his cart with Sarah up the elevator to our extravagant suite overlooking Central Park.

As soon as we entered our room, Sarah darted toward the bathroom and started drawing warm water into the bathtub—while ripping her clothes off. She looked angry, and once the tub had a couple inches of water in it, I noticed she was crouched under the spigot, uncontrollably splashing warm water over her womb.

While Sarah was tweaking, I stashed my cash in the closet, rolled the baggage cart back into the hallway, and fell back flat onto the bed. As I stared up at the ceiling, I could hear the background sounds of moaning and running water echoing in the bathroom. *How the fuck did I get myself into this situation?* I thought to myself. I knew how, though. I was blinded by the sex, and now that I had been wrangled in by it, I was being used as a pawn in a game—Sarah's game of crying to get my attention, making me feel like I'd done something wrong, and then getting me to submit to her desires. Meanwhile, she'd take my own words and twist them around so they were barely recognizable to me. So much so that I'd find myself speechless at times, because she knew precisely how to confuse me and make me seem crazy, while she played victim, leaving me feeling like I'd caused the problems she cleverly created.

Yeah, of course I was part of the problem, but at this point in my life, I thought everyone else was the problem.

"I'm ordering some wasabi prawns and a yellowtail roll. Do you want anything?" I asked Sarah, through the cracked-open bathroom door.

"How about you order some respect for your girlfriend?

You're a drug dealer and all you care about is money," she shrieked back.

"Shhh, you're gonna wake the neighbors."

I could tell another one of her episodes was brewing. She was still moaning in the bathtub, but I didn't know if she was serious because she cried wolf every other day. *Oh Jill, where are you?* I thought. Jill was tough and self-sufficient. She wouldn't have acted like this, and for a moment, I thought I should've just bought Jill the ring and the white picket fence.

When Sarah came out of the bathroom, she had one towel wrapped around her torso and one wrapped around her hair. She started raising her voice and I started getting nervous because it was after midnight, and if any neighbors heard it, they might consider it a domestic dispute and call security. I also knew, in the heat of the moment, Sarah would happily tell security I had cash stashed in the closet. It'd be her way of sharing her pain with me, because she was a slave to her emotions. She was certified bipolar.

"You're a fucking asshole and you're lucky you're not in jail!" Sarah snapped, in a scary tone.

"Please calm down," I begged.

I could tell she was about to explode, and within seconds she did a tornado spin and gave me a slap to the face.

Acting on instinct, I grabbed her wrists and pinned her to the bed, face down. I couldn't allow things to escalate. I was trapped by over forty floors and floor-to-ceiling windows that would've made it impossible for me to escape safely with two hundred pounds of cash, without police questioning. My only option was to talk her through it while restraining her.

"Please calm down. I love you. I promise we'll keep the next one. We'll start a family," I lied into her ear, with her face in the pillow.

Sarah lifted her face from the pillow. "Really? I want to get married. I want to be together forever," she whimpered.

I released her wrists, and within seconds we were kissing.

I felt like I was living in a horror film. I think the Adderall and Xanax had seized control of Sarah's mind. It seemed Adderall boosted her mood, but once it wore off, her anxiety and depression would kick in at both of our expenses. So much so that she'd take Xanax to relax. It was a roller coaster, and there was never time for a normal conversation. I wanted to help her, but I didn't know how, and at this very moment I wasn't about to let her call 9-1-1. Instead, I needed her to feel hopeful, immediately. Because if she thought there was a possibility of a better future between us, it'd calm her down and give me time to think of a permanent solution to us when I was more rested.

14

HELD HOSTAGE

I t was the week before our LA film shoot, and Henry, my lead cameraman for *A Woman's Mind*, was the person responsible for relaying messages from me to our production manager. Henry was trustworthy, about five-foot-ten, stocky, and eight years my senior. He was overwhelmed by the amount of cash I was spending, having already witnessed me blow over two million bucks on my crew, travel, girls, parties, and fuck-ups.

"Henry, I need a modern luxury home with enough room to dance in. I want a DJ, a full bar, and a competent bartender," I said over the phone one afternoon in 2007. "I also need an ice luge, a pool table, a hot tub, and some hot servers, to pass around hors d'oeuvres. Don't forget about the Rolls and the limo to bring the girls to the party. Okay?"

"Sure, boss! What about an animal? You want a lion? A tiger?" Henry asked.

"Not this time. Please just make sure the camera batteries are charged. No fuck-ups. Okay?"

My film crew was a headache. I was constantly reminding them how to do their job. I wanted to hire an established production house, but I couldn't because I paid for my production in cash and I didn't want to raise any red flags. The benefit of my underqualified crew was that I felt confident they'd keep their lips sealed and never rat me out.

As I approached our LA house party, I saw a gorgeous woman on the porch bent down, cooing over several white Huskies, as her breasts were spilling from her pink sparkly top. Apparently Henry had decided to get the animals. I wondered how much I was paying for that scene.

When I entered the house, women were grinding to 2Pac's "I Get Around," thumping through the DJ's PA system set up in the main room, and servers in miniskirts were passing around hors d'oeuvres. Through the large glass windows, I could see four beautiful women on the back deck, naked, in the hot tub. I wanted to jump in, but I couldn't because I had to direct my film crew. I had to at every party, and they were a regular occurrence in each city at the end of each day I interviewed women.

As I stood at the house bar, I was envisioning how I was going to get out of the weed game, become a TV show host, and facilitate happy relationships. That's when a redhead with dark red lipstick, who I'd interviewed earlier, approached me and whispered over the rim of her martini glass, "If she treats you like a joke, you should laugh, and then leave her like it's funny."

I chuckled and smiled. She knew Sarah was interfering with my project. She studied clinical psychology, and had witnessed Sarah's erratic behavior on the film set earlier that day.

"So why are you filming this?" she asked, keeping her gaze locked on me.

"I want to prevent divorce."

"I don't think that's all you're up to," she said, using her free hand to twist her hair.

I smiled and leaned back on the bar, checking out her figure as she crossed her legs toward me. She knew what she was doing; she wanted Sarah's spot.

"I live a life most people wouldn't understand," I said.

"I doubt that. I think you live a life *you* don't understand."

I smiled again and replied with confidence, "What I understand is that people want what they don't have. So if I create this show in lavish settings. People who've never experienced them will watch—no matter what the premise is. These expensive settings will be my lure to feed viewers' insights that may save their marriages."

Suddenly, a pull on my right arm spun me partially around.

"Eric! Henry and Stix aren't filming. They're double-teaming one of the girls downstairs. They should've been fired by now!" Sarah shouted.

Stix was my film editor, and stood somewhere between a hopeless romantic and a sex addict. I probably should have fired him, but I never knew what to believe when Sarah spoke because I'd witnessed her trample so many people to advance herself. I had to keep her around, though. It was important that I kept her satisfied until my production was done. After that, my plan was to claim I was useless, that I'd run out of money, and the film footage was garbage. It would be a drawn-out process for her to buy the story, but once she assumed I was a dead end, she'd strategically move onto her next victim.

This wasn't my favorite course of action, but like Jim always told me: "Patience is a form of action."

To appease Sarah, I left the bar and walked downstairs to check on my film crew. They were nowhere to be found, so I reached into my pocket and fished out my Palm Treo. As I was about to call them, I saw a disturbing text on my screen that read, "Pay up, or it's an 8' x 8' for you." Attached to the message was a photo of a pile of weed from my warehouse in Saratoga. My stomach dropped. *That motherfucker,* I thought. It was a young distant relative of mine who was hard up, whom I'd hired out of kindness to weigh and package weed, and who was now trying to blackmail me with the threat of a jail cell. On top of that, he texted the incriminating evidence from his personal phone to my personal phone, which was attached to both our names and could potentially cause irreversible damage. I couldn't believe it.

I took a deep breath, went into a quiet back room, and called the young kid from one of my burners.

"You fuck!" I growled. "What's your problem?" But I already knew why he was pissed. I had fired him for not showing up to work one too many times, when I had deadlines to meet.

"I'm not the one with a problem—you are," he replied.

I gritted my teeth. The little punk thought he was the mob. "If you're testing my waters—"

"Now you know I'm serious," he said, cutting me off coolly, with no fear in his voice.

Anger ran through me. "I'll be back in town tomorrow. Wait for my call."

I didn't sleep a wink that night, and on my flight home, I went over my three options. I could pay him, in which case he'd know I was weak and that he could do it again. I could not pay him, in which case he'd possibly tip off the cops. And there was a third option, one that I couldn't believe even crossed my mind. I could make him disappear. Permanently.

One of my associates in the past had told me that he could get me a "hammer" if I ever needed one. But I never acknowledged the offer, because I was a nonviolent boss. My weapon of choice was my calm mind. I handled things diplomatically. I didn't need a gun to enforce anything. I was honorable in my dealings, but I was furious now. Furious that my employee didn't notice all the things I'd done for him, until I stopped doing them. And when I stopped, he tweaked and threatened me with prison. Still, I couldn't hurt him. I'd never touched a gun outside of the range, and I didn't plan to now, because nonviolence was my policy.

THE FOLLOWING day I pulled into my driveway on a secluded parcel of land in Saratoga. I immediately noticed the lock to my cargo trailer had been cut off, and my jaw dropped. I threw my truck in park, ran toward the trailer, and looked inside. It was empty. Someone had stolen $600,000 worth of weed from me while I was in LA.

I clenched my fists. Less than a handful of people knew where I lived, and my packager was the immediate suspect.

I took a deep breath, reached into my messenger bag, and popped a battery into my burner, labeled "P" for Packagers.

"Where the fuck are you?" I asked my former packager.

"I'm around. You back in town?"

"Yes!" I said, with fury. "Come to my house—now!"

It wasn't my modus operandi to store weed near my private residence, but I didn't have time to move it to the stash house before leaving town.

It's safe to say, the filming of A Woman's Mind had officially started compromising other areas of my life. A life I was spreading thin, and a life that was getting messy. My days were blurring together, because I was the king of doing too much. I didn't have time to take a deep breath, and I didn't even realize it. The only thing I knew was what a European escort once told me: "America is known as the place where you work until you die."

When my packager arrived, I was fuming.

"Where is it?" I asked, right in his face.

"Where's what?" he answered, without a flinch.

"The half-million dollars worth of grass you stole from me!"

Right then, I knew he didn't do it. When I saw his face freeze and hands twitch, I knew he was scared for his life. He only wanted the three thousand he claimed I owed him for firing him. Only three grand! I couldn't believe it. The amount didn't matter, though; it was the principle.

I actually felt bad for the kid. For a second, he had the same face I'd had, when Jim gave me nowhere to run.

"I'll give you the three now, but if I find out you stole from me or you come around again—"

Suddenly, a burner rang in my back pocket, interrupting us.

"Yo," I answered.

"You back?" Streets asked. "I need my order," he said, accompanied by a cough.

I could tell he'd just cleared a bong hit as I pinned the burner between my right ear and shoulder and reached for cash in my front pocket to pay my packager.

"Yeah, I'm back. But someone robbed me while I was out of town."

"I told you to quit that stupid TV show. You're gonna go broke trying to look rich."

I remained silent for a moment, counting out the hundreds in my hand. "I'll have your order for you in two days. I have more on the way," I said.

"Say less, do more!" Streets replied.

I thought twice before deciding not to respond. Streets was right. My film production was robbing me of my mental strength. I'd been selling weed for over a decade and I was beginning to act without thinking. The fast money was taking me out of line with my true self, and my poor choices were now resulting in expensive losses and enormous frustration. I had created a life of obligations that was dragging me along so fast that most of my decisions were being made on autopilot. I had too many people around me; more than I had time for. I was assisting family members when they needed money, spending time with friends when they complained I didn't hang out anymore, and attending pointless events I was invited to. I think I kept so many people around because I was subconsciously afraid to go back to living life alone. Either way, I needed to start pruning people from my life, because like Mom often said, "Show me your friends, and I'll tell you your future."

Mom was smart, but before I could start cutting people out of my life, I first needed to bug sweep all my houses and cars, to verify if I was or wasn't being investigated by the government. I started thinking dirty cops may have robbed me, because I'd heard stories of them conducting legitimate investigations while secretly tipping off third parties to the whereabouts of a suspected drug dealer's inventory—so it could be stolen, resold, and the proceeds split.

Luckily, all my sweeps came up clean, but just in case, I switched out all my stash houses and all my burners. I also wrote off the hit as a loss, and as I pushed onward, I kept all my next moves to myself. And sure enough, my strategic moves slowly took a toll on my soul, and I became more tired every day. However, that didn't stop me. I just kept pushing forward, which only enhanced the problem by overriding my normal sleep pattern. And when I lacked sleep, it was difficult for me to focus. And as we all know, and as Jim always said, "Your focus will determine your reality."

15

AUTHENTICITY

I t'd been a couple years since I'd taken a vacation, but since Sarah was away visiting friends in Spain for a few weeks, it was an opportune time for me to escape to Belize with Rob. I was only going for a couple nights to clear my head and view some property an associate of mine had for sale. The goal was to research options for moving some of my cash offshore, because hidden assets, secret accounts, and invisible money is how I'd protect myself from a government attack.

The first night in Belize, we found ourselves riding down a dirt road surrendering to the power of hallucinogenic mushrooms. We'd discreetly mixed them into our sushi at a local restaurant and then attempted to drive back to our rental property.

While sitting in the passenger seat of our SUV rental, everything around me was undulating with ripples. When I looked out the window to my right, I could see low-lying vegetation and a man on a rickety bicycle, heading in the same direction as us, actually passing us on the shoulder of the dusty road. I blinked to make sure he was real, and yep, Rob was driving around six miles per hour and the biker was advancing past us with little effort.

"D...D..Dude!" I stuttered, uncontrollably laughing.

Rob remained focused intently on the road, but his blank face eventually looked over to me, and neither of us could say a complete word. We just both started laughing with tears streaming down our faces, driving even slower than before, to the point where we stopped for a minute, thinking we were stuck in traffic, except there wasn't a car around us as far as the eye could see.

My imagination was running wild, and I liked it. It was the ultimate escape.

After taking what seemed like an hour to drive two miles, we finally arrived at our rental house. It was a beautiful bungalow nestled among wild tropical foliage, with a backdrop of the deep blue ocean. Still laughing, we settled into a string of hammocks, lining the perimeter of the porch, overlooking the beach. The sky was slashed with pink and orange, and as the shrooms intensified, the mood shifted and we became quiet.

Positioned comfortably in my hammock, I honed in on the rhythm of the waves. The tempo was soothing. I began to acknowledge that my best moments in life were always unplanned, and as I felt my system unlock and the stress pour out of me, I fully relaxed in oneness for the first time since I didn't know when. Everything felt more authentic than my regular everyday life, and as the sun went down, I stared into the abyss, watching the stars pop out, one by one. That's when I shouted out, "I'm done!"

"What, Lips?" Rob asked.

I snapped my head up, forgetting Rob was on the porch across from me. I thought I was alone. I was engrossed in thinking about how far I'd made it in the weed game, and that it was time to retire. Something didn't feel right anymore. It was a gut feeling I didn't always trust, but always should have. It was the feeling that often revolved around my hardest decision—whether to give up or try harder.

The facts were: It was 2008, I was twenty-nine, and I had sold close to $300 million worth of weed since my first deal. All without a gun, violence, or the government knowing. I was quite surprised by my math, but the more I thought about it, I realized I'd bought and sold a combined total of over a half-billion dollars worth of weed, and now the shrooms were advising me to quit dealing—immediately.

"I want out. It doesn't feel right anymore," I replied to Rob.

"I've been telling you to quit for years, but you always say you're not quitting until you get caught. Why are you still in?"

A bubble started forming in my chest. I could never hide from the truth on psychedelics. They made me confront myself, and I couldn't hold back the stream of tears that erupted from me seconds after Rob asked the question.

"She . . . she . . . she told me I'd never make it," I sputtered between the tears and gasping breaths.

I twisted myself upright in the hammock. I could see a dark outline of Rob across the porch, as tears continued streaming down my face. They were coming from a pain so deep I'd forgotten it was there—probably because my life was so busy. But right then, I knew my body hadn't forgotten. I was trembling, and Rob didn't say a word. He just let me pour it out. He knew my ego needed work . . . but he didn't understand *why*, because he had never witnessed my childhood quarrels. The only true witness to that was my heart, which I'd been avoiding for years.

"Lips, are you okay?" Rob asked, as I came back around.

"Yeah, I'm good. You want my weed business?"

"Ahhhh—" Rob paused. "I don't want it, but I'll help you with it."

I must have still been tripping, because the business was too big for him to run solo anyway. There were too many delicate relationships and emotions for any one person to maintain on their own without losing themselves in the process. The only reason I could do it was because I had sacrificed the other areas of life needed to maintain balance. It would've taken a few people to run my company, and I couldn't exactly place an ad on CareerBuilder. Although the more I thought about it, I thought Streets could handle one portion of my business and Rob could handle the other. Regardless, I needed to scale the business down before I sold it to anyone—which would be a fairly easy task, since it was already slowing on its own because one of my suppliers had recently been indicted in a federal case with a $250 million judgment.

Since then, my inventory had been lacking. Plus, it was 2008, the year California's illicit weed operations multiplied rapidly, and larger amounts of its lower-priced weed were being dispersed along the East Coast. This low-cost option was flooding the market and my customers began complaining my prices were too high. It seemed every possible signal was alerting me that my run was over. I think it was the universe trying to pull me on the correct path, like a river. A river that seemed to put me where I was supposed to be when I flowed with it, and a river that seemed to drown me when I fought it.

16

HOLLYWOOD

"Baby, I'm going to hit the spa before I network at the event this afternoon," Sarah said from the bathroom of our hotel room.

We were staying at Shutters on the Beach Hotel, in Santa Monica, to attend the American Film Market conference, in order to familiarize ourselves with the film industry—something I should've done before I started my circus production.

"Okay, but please don't spend too much at the spa," I replied.

Little statements like this were part of my plan to get her to think money was getting tight. I'd already told her I'd blown most of my savings on the film and that I needed to sell the project quickly or I wouldn't be able to afford to renew our house lease. And as anticipated, she was slowly shifting her attention away from me, because I've found there's one way to get your partner to leave your life—make them want to leave.

After Sarah walked out the door, I pulled up Eros.com on my laptop. It was my go-to worldwide guide to escorts. There were plenty of women to choose from in the LA vicinity, but the quality wasn't matching the refined New York City selections I was accustomed to, and as I scrolled down further, my disappointment grew. But then I saw "Summer," a globe-strutting model with a penchant for refined gentlemen. Selective, sophisticated, independent, and a co-creator of remarkable adventures.

Bingo! I was sold.

I immediately dialed her number. When she answered in a seductive tone, we chatted briefly, and after I quickly passed her verification process, we set up a rendezvous for later that evening—when Sarah would be out networking for her next boyfriend.

I chatted with Summer for another minute, but I had to cut it short to take another call I had coming in.

"Yo," I answered.

"Where are you?" Streets asked.

"On my beach balcony, overlooking the Pacific."

"Are you looking at samples?" he asked.

"No, I'm in LA for my show. I'll make another trip out next week, though," I replied, knowing that earlier in the week I'd told Streets I'd soon be going to Northern Cali to look at weed samples from several suppliers and farmers I knew.

"Grow up and stop the show! Stop seeking attention!" Streets shouted.

"Relax, things are lined up for next week. I'll have some good news for you, too."

I planned to sell part of my weed business to Streets in installments, because I believed in him and I knew he could keep it profitable.

Streets was persistent. He was the one person who could uphold my reputation. He was also relentless, sometimes to the point of irritating, but those are usually the type of people who are the most confident and set the standard in any organization. They don't accept failure, and they always have to be active in something, like Streets, who was a warrior and ready to take on the world every day. Most importantly, he could adapt to change quickly, and he never made excuses. Plus, he'd take full responsibility if anything ever went wrong, because he was a true leader.

I SPENT the remainder of the day networking at the event as my film crew passed out my DVD trailer, generated buzz, and fetched leads. It seemed like every time I was handed a business card, I got pitched that they were the best thing since sliced bread. Everyone said they were less than three degrees of separation away from the person who was going to make all my dreams a reality. The meet and greets were fast, and I couldn't tell if it was the coffee or the yayo that kept them talking my ear off, because I wasn't paying close attention—not until Henry came up to me and said, "People have been asking who you are and how you can afford yacht parties and shit. What should I say?"

I wasn't sure how to respond. My film crew had no idea I smuggled weed. I told them I'd made my money in my water feature business, but I later found out they thought I smuggled immigrants over the Canadian border. They came to this conclusion because I once cracked a joke about how I could smuggle anyone into the country for eight grand. I hadn't realized they'd taken me seriously, so I didn't have a valid answer for Henry. I just said, "Tell them I'm an entrepreneur."

Above all the chatter at the event, I did meet a few solid players who admired my project. One of them was part of a small, connected, up-and-coming production house, who later went on to create and produce the popular Netflix series *Ozark*. We had a good conversation, so the following day I made time for a closed-door meeting with him and his team, at their office, in a small building somewhere in Santa Monica. The room we met in had lots of windows perfectly positioned to allow the Cali sunshine to bounce off the table and sweeten up any deals discussed there.

"Eric, we watched your video clips. We think you're onto something," said the partner of the boutique studio.

A wave of gratification ran through me.

"Thank you. What in particular did you like about the clips?" I replied, as I absorbed his compliment and settled into a leather chair at the sleek conference table.

"It's hard to get women to open up on camera. You made them forget they were being filmed. That's a skill you could be compensated for. We think you have what it takes to have your own show. Trust me, every prom king and queen in the country moves to LA, hoping to make it big, but they end up bartending. You're different, though."

Right then, I got that winning feeling. It felt like all my unseen victories I'd had in the past were finally going to lead me to something big. I felt like I could finally show Mom and the world I'd made it. Probably because I was raised to believe that success is based on a job, a house, and money. And I believed in the illusion that all these things would make me feel whole and complete—and with that belief came frustration, as there always seemed to be a better job, a nicer house, and more money to be had.

The studio immediately wanted to initiate talks with Bravo TV on my behalf, and partner up with me if the numbers worked, but I wasn't sure if I could handle the limelight yet. Henry reminded me I'd eventually have to explain where I'd come up with the money to film what I'd already done, and that a major network show could put my outlaw activities directly in the Fed's crosshairs. So I told the studio I was interested but that I needed time to wrap up some unfinished business in New York before they started spinning their wheels for deals.

It was imperative to completely remove myself from the weed game before attempting a new career.

WHEN I STEPPED out of the meeting that was going to make all my dreams come true, I saw a missed call from Summer, and with a smile on my face, I dialed her number, hoping she'd answer.

"Hey, did you call me?" I asked, when Summer answered.

"Yeah, honey. Unfortunately, I'm feeling under the weather, but my friend said she'd be willing to meet you, and she's stunning. Trust me."

Yeah, right. Racket, I thought.

"Send me some pics of her," I requested, apprehensively.

"I don't have any pics of her, and she isn't on the web. She hasn't done this before, so you have to promise you'll be nice to her."

A feeling of frustration immediately ran through me, but I needed a release. Sex with Sarah had ceased since my "useless" front went into effect, and considering the address Summer gave me was only a couple miles from my hotel, I didn't have much to lose. Therefore, I agreed to meet Summer's friend later that evening. I had hoped it would be a good break from my normal life—or I should say, not so normal. Either way, there is no normal life—there's just life—and I was doing whatever the fuck I wanted in it. I was doing what made me feel most alive, because my life revolved around adventure. It was about seeing and feeling everything, rather than reading or hearing about it.

AS MY CAB pulled up to the address Summer had given me, I couldn't make out if anyone was inside. The unlit bungalow was small, with a dim street light reflecting off the empty narrow driveway beside it. There weren't any cars parked in the driveway or on the street in front, and when the cab took off, I was left alone on the sidewalk.

I took a minute to collect myself before I walked up onto the covered wooden porch and gently knocked on the door, and within seconds, the door quietly opened, and holy Cupid, I was in love. Her aura was glowing with life. I felt like I'd just walked into the Garden of Eden. Her hair had an oily shine. She had the body of a Pilates instructor, and her face was straight off the cover of *Vanity Fair*. She was the most beautiful woman I'd ever met—beautiful as in born with good genetics.

"Hi, you must be, Eric," she said, reaching out for a gentle handshake, locking eyes with me.

"Hi, you must be Ava," I replied, clasping her hand with both of mine, as I leaned in and placed a kiss on her cheek. "Summer speaks highly of you," I added.

"Oh, Summer, she's so sweet," Ava replied, as she gently locked the door behind me.

I stepped directly into what seemed to be the living room. The room was small, some jazzy blues were quietly playing through a laptop, and three pillar candles provided the only light. There was no couch or any personal items, just a queen bed with freshly washed sheets, a fluffy taupe-colored comforter, and a small white fur rug at the edge of the bed. The laptop sat on a small IKEA desk, acting as a nightstand, with a matching contemporary chair pulled up in front of it. I could hear my footsteps echo off the barren walls, as I walked across the old hardwood floor, toward the bed. I assumed the other two rooms were empty, because it was obvious that this house was for sex only. It was perfectly staged for secret encounters with clients who passed Summer's basic screening, and were willing to shell out two thousand and up.

"Would you like some?" Ava asked, holding up a bottle of red in one hand.

"Sure," I said, but I didn't need the social lubricant, because I finally knew how to navigate the bedroom with breath and confidence. But since I could see nervousness in Ava's eyes, I assumed the only way to calm her was to share the liquid courage.

After chatting about LA life over a glass of wine, I definitely knew this was Ava's first time as a working girl, because she still hadn't asked for money. She was lost in the moment. I think she was enjoying my company. She said I was charming, and what really made her melt was when I showed her the trailer for my web series on her laptop.

"Wow! You're really going to make it with this," she said, placing her glass on the desk, and then gently placing herself next to me on the edge of the bed as she continued on with, "I feel weird doing this. You know, meeting you under these conditions. I really like you."

Right then, I knew she felt safe with me, and I replied, "I feel the same," while placing my left hand below the small of her back.

Ava smelled clean. She didn't need any perfume. Her pheromones could've hooked a blue marlin, and now that I had the green light, I brushed my right hand past her ear and into her long, straight, highlighted hair. When our lips touched, I could feel her spirit run down my spine, through my heart, and straight to my balls. Fuck, I was ready to start a family at the incall location of a boutique escort operation. I don't think Mom would've approved.

As I took Ava's clothes off, I felt the most sacred intimacy I had ever experienced. When she gripped me, it felt like she needed to be rescued from something. Her breasts were perfect, and I could almost close my hands around her slim waist. There was no way she was an escort; she was more the type to take lunch dates at Cafe Gratitude. She was pure . . . and when she guided me in, it felt like I'd been plugged into the strongest energy field on earth. Like I'd passed all the tests and was allowed to progress to the next level. Our bodies meshed like yin and yang. For a second, I thought maybe as one we could fulfill all our dreams together. Sure, maybe I was delusional and we were just excited to be breaking the law, but either way, after we touched all five senses, we orgasmed simultaneously and it was heaven. Actually, it was therapeutic, and I craved the immediate numbness that permeated my mind as I slowly rolled off her and shared the afterglow in silence, on our backs, side by side, with our arms touching. I felt like our souls knew each other.

Ava was priming me for round two when we noticed my silenced Palm Treo ceaselessly lighting up my jeans pocket on the floor.

"Sorry, I have to check who's calling," I said, turning toward Ava's ear.

"Eric, there's a party you should come to," I barely made out through my phone. I could hear a lot of background noise, as my entertainment attorney, Stan, shouted: "Where are you?"

Stan was my plug into the film industry. He was a "Super Lawyer," and had played a nurturing role in many artists' careers, including Britney Spears, Taylor Swift, and Lady Gaga.

"I'm at a friend's, in Santa Monica. Where's the party?" I asked.

"I'm driving around Santa Monica now with a buddy. What's your address? We'll pick you up."

I gave Stan the address a couple houses down the street, out of courtesy for Summer's illicit business. But I was torn . . . I didn't want to leave Ava, and when I saw four missed calls from Sarah, I really didn't want to leave.

As Ava overheard my call with Stan, she reached toward the

desk and wrote her personal number down on a sliver of paper. When my call ended, I pulled my pants on and stood up. Ava stood up too, pulled me in close, and slipped her phone number into my hand while looking me straight in the eye and saying, "You're gonna call me, right?"

"You know I will," I replied, lovingly. "How much do I owe you?"

"Nothing, just make sure I see you soon. Okay?" she said, squeezing my wrists, reaching up on her toes to give me a kiss in her tiny panties.

I would've felt guilty not paying, so I dropped several hundreds on the desk before turning to the door.

WHILE STANDING on the quiet street waiting for Stan, I remembered one of the women I interviewed had said, "Money's a man's makeup," and for a second, I wondered if Ava would've opened up to me without my flashy videos. I knew my fat wallet drew women to me, but without it, what was my value? Some would say I was cool, some would say I was handsome, and some would say I was confident. But I knew those features were enhanced by my cash, just like the women who enhance their lips with gloss and their eyes with liner. The question was, was I hiding behind my money, and what do others hide behind? Do they name-drop because they're insecure? Are they angry because they don't think the world loves them? Are they in debt with shiny toys to prove something? . . . I didn't know. I just assumed some people wear these masks out of fear that others may find out who they really are. At least I did, and at times I had on so many masks that I actually forgot who I was. Fuck, what an exhausting way to live. I was somewhere between giving up and seeing how much more I could take.

. . .

I WAS TAKEN ABACK as I witnessed Stan pull up in a beat-up 1984 Chrysler Lebaron Town & Country convertible. The top was down, wood paneling wrapped the exterior, and only one hubcap remained. The shocks and struts were clearly shot, because the car was sitting crooked and way too low. The driver looked like he rejected all the social customs associated with Hollywood. He was a textbook hippie, and I could smell remnants of smoked weed emitting from his ashtray.

"Hop in," Stan said, in his crisp blazer and designer jeans, promptly introducing me to his buddy, "The Dude," whom I soon found out was the basis for Jeff Bridges' famous role in *The Big Lebowski*.

"Nice to meet you, Dude," I said, reaching up from the back seat, with a firm handshake to his relaxed hand.

The Dude cranked his stereo up over the loud muffler as we rolled off listening to Joe Cocker's "Feeling Alright," through one front speaker, which rattled the interior door panel each time the bass struck. The three other speakers were blown, but one was just enough to keep my spirits on cloud nine as the wind blew through my hair and I fantasized about which tropical island I'd take Ava to when Sarah finally left me.

"Stan tells me you're filming some women," The Dude said. We were stopped at a red light as he passed back a simple business card that read "Jeff Dowd," along with his contact information.

I didn't want to carry on a conversation over his loud car, so I just replied, "Yeah, I'm trying to understand women's emotions."

The Dude and Stan both laughed, and I smiled back.

I actually was learning quite a bit from my film. It made me realize I didn't have the time to solely give any one woman what she most likely wanted: patience, understanding, empathy, and compassion. Because for me, time was money, and it was more efficient to buy a woman's time than to give her my time. When I paid for a woman's time, it was like going to a restaurant, looking at the menu, and picking out exactly what I wanted. No bullshit, no baggage, and no broken hearts. I'd get what I paid for. I probably would've become more emotional if I found a woman who supported my present and encouraged my future, but my options were limited in the underworld. I must admit, though, my romantic lifestyle became lonely at times—especially when I ate alone at my favorite restaurants.

ONCE STAN CLEARED us with the doorman, I realized we were at Harvey Weinstein's party—which was glitzy. All the women's dresses were short and tight, and some were sparkling more than the champagne. I could actually feel the "pick *me*" vibe running through the air. It seemed everyone was in a glorified waiting room, waiting to be noticed and picked for the next best role, and the next best award. It then registered, these were all the prom kings and queens the studio head was talking about. Most were tall and had good facial symmetry, high cheekbones, and eyes that stood out. All the features necessary to keep the masses' attention. Features that make money and that would be used in American films, which would spread American culture around the world. Fuck, this was it . . . I was smack-dab in the middle of where hopes, dreams, and desires would be assembled and eventually exported to all corners of the globe via big-budget Hollywood films.

After a few minutes of mingling, I unexpectedly bumped into a minor buzzkill: Sarah. She was able to weasel her way into the party with some guy she already had drooling.

"Eric, meet my new friend Kevin. He's a phenomenal producer," Sarah said, in a drunken giggle. "He just completed funding for his upcoming film," she added, pulling me in to shake his hand.

"Nice to meet you, Kevin," I said, with a firm handshake and big smile, specifically repeating his name back to him, hoping the sound of it would comfort him and relay confidence that he had my permission to take Sarah home—preferably forever.

As I drifted away from the two of them toward the far back corner of the party, I discreetly checked a burner for my New Orleans customer that'd been vibrating in my pocket with a new text message alert.

"Code Red!" blared on the screen.

I stopped dead in my tracks, standing in the main causeway of the party, with people sliding past me on both sides. I then instantly pulled another burner out of my pocket, the one for my driver who was en route to deliver a million-dollar load to my suddenly endangered New Orleans customer, and texted: CODE RED! CODE RED! TURN AROUND NOW! COME HOME! PLEASE, CALL ME!

I immediately rushed out of the party and onto the sidewalk. I frantically ripped the battery out of my New Orleans burner, broke the flip screen from the keypad, wiped my fingerprints off all three parts with my shirt, and threw each part in a different direction—one across the street, another in the dumpster behind the club, and the last in the garbage can on the corner. "Code Red" meant cops were onto my customer and that I shouldn't be in possession of a phone tied to him. I could only hope my driver would get my emergency text, before getting too close to New Orleans with the load.

My driver had a separate burner for the customer as well, and I prayed none of our burners had already been pinged by the Feds, which is the first step in any DEA investigation. Location, location, location.

I walked back into the party, because I didn't want Stan to think I'd ghosted him. And when I eventually spotted him standing in the distance, I beelined it toward him to say goodbye, as my heart was racing with uncertainty and my driver's burner clenched in the palm of my hand, waiting for a reply.

"Yo, Amigo . . . thank you for inviting me," I said to Stan, politely interrupting him, talking to a blonde. "I gotta roll out," I added, giving him a firm shoulder grip, trying not to break up his conversation.

"Hold on, there's someone I want you to meet," Stan said, quickly spinning himself around. "Harvey, this is Eric. He's the guy interviewing all the women."

Harvey Weinstein looked haggard. I could see the exhaustion in his face, probably from spreading himself too thin. It was obvious he entertained a lot of people. I assumed he was losing himself among them, too, probably in order to keep them happy. I could relate, because it was happening to me, just on a much smaller scale. Having too many friends, playing multiple roles at multiple social obligations, and being the "person you call" was draining me. Why? Because when you're in the spotlight you have to constantly maintain your self-image—sometimes to the point where no one knows the true you. Not even yourself.

I did feel honored when Harvey said, "I'd love to see what you're working on," even though he felt like a gatekeeper to my success—mostly because I assumed his mood would determine whether or not my show made it to the masses. And I hated that feeling, because I struggled with gatekeepers. But I still told Harvey I'd have Stan relay some of my edited footage to him in a couple months—even though my ego wasn't interested in his help, mainly because I wanted to be recognized for making it on my own, by partnering with the small production company, which would hopefully allow me to have a voice in the creative process. Plus, going from the role of a boss to someone's puppet wasn't an option for me.

Of course, my fat ego was in the way, but I was adamant that Mom would be the last person to ever have control over my destiny. And I'm sure this mentality prevented me from flourishing in many ways, but unfortunately I was trapped in my history and my history was trapped in me.

My conversation was brief with Harvey, because a tall brunette was seeking his attention and I was itching to check my burner. So once the brunette successfully hijacked his ear, I slipped out the door, saw a missed call from my driver, and instantly called him back. Thankfully he was safe at a hotel in the Carolinas, which was a relief to hear, and allowed me to instruct him to immediately destroy his burner connecting him to the New Orleans drop-point, and to meet me back in Saratoga the following night for a status update—the type you can't post on Facebook.

17

CHOICES

The following month, I found out my New Orleans customer was tipped off about a developing investigation into him, so he fled the country. I'm not sure what his exit strategy was, because I never heard from him again. At least he disappeared properly without a trace, I thought. I also never found out who robbed me, but with my potential opportunity in Hollywood, and the fact that Sarah had finally moved to Chicago, it was all water under the bridge.

I remained friends with Sarah, and I could finally put my plan to downsize, restructure, and exit the weed business into hyperdrive. My first step was to cut out the customers who didn't pay on time and haggled over price. My second step was to source less from my expensive Canadian connects and set up a small pipeline from Cali to New York, which Rob would manage, by sourcing and packaging all my orders in Cali, and then shipping them directly to Streets in Brooklyn, New York. My third step would be to give Streets my best customers on the East Coast, so I could say, "Hello, pension," and "Ava, will you ride with me?"

. . .

AFTER I'D PUT some feelers out in California for wholesale weed options, I lasered in on one that I particularly liked. My only problem was, I didn't feel comfortable having any of my drivers transporting cash to the West Coast and weed to the East Coast. Mostly because my organization lacked the necessary experience in cross-country transport. After some more thought, though, I realized I had a customer who'd be the perfect driver to blend into the remote roads in Northern California. She was a former world champion downhill mountain biker, and it just so happened that mountain biking originated in North California, very close to my weed pickup location. I assumed she'd have no problem talking to law enforcement in that region. They may have even asked for her autograph, because she was one of mountain biking's first mainstream superstars, known for winning several World Cups, being on the cover of magazines, and being a guest on talk shows. Her name was Missy Giove. She was an athletic surfer type with long, black, wavy hair, and a fast talker who could charm anyone out of a black hole. She was also a regular customer of mine who consigned around a half-million per month for distribution in St. Louis, Missouri, and over the past two years, she had regularly asked to be one of my fill-in drivers, but I usually declined, wary of her overt flattery.

"BABY, let me know if you need any routes done. You're so easy to work with," Missy said on a crisp fall day, as she transferred cash from the trunk of her Cadillac DeVille into the cab of my truck.

We were on a secluded piece of land in Saratoga and the cash was from her customer in St. Louis.

"I have a higher-risk California run that pays sixty grand, if you're interested—"

"I'll do it! You know I'm here for you, baby," Missy replied, cutting me off.

Her rapid-fire voice left me unconvinced that she'd actually heard what I said, and I wanted to see deeper into her, but her sunglasses were on and she was covered in tattoos.

"Listen, this is the longest run in the country, which means more cops and more room for error," I explained, hoping my words would stick.

My rules were made clear to all my drivers. They needed to be clean-cut, blend in with traffic, and no driving before 8 a.m. or after 9 p.m. with out-of-state plates. Most importantly, they couldn't have a criminal record—although this Cali run required additional precautions, and I needed Missy's undivided attention.

"You'll need to buy a cargo trailer that can fit a minimum of five hundred pounds, plus all your mountain bikes," I said, further explaining that her cover story was that she was traveling across the country to shoot videos for a Mini Mountain Bike Series. There would be a lot of visible biking paraphernalia in the cab of her truck, her cargo trailer needed to be professionally wrapped with the logo of her film project, and her bikes needed to be in the trailer among the crates of weed. In Cali, Rob would load the crates of weed into her trailer and the "story" would be that they contained her film equipment. The setup would be discreet, believable, and safe. "Is anything unclear?" I asked.

"I understand, baby. I know the rules. You know I'm solid. My dad was a bookie for the Mob. If I go down, my lips are sealed," Missy replied, trying to ease my nerves.

Missy kept me on edge, but she said more than once that if she got busted she'd do her time before snitching, and I believed her because she came across as fearless, the type of person who would do anything for the team. I figured the worst that could happen would be a million-dollar load lost on the road and some hefty attorney fees. But at this point, I didn't really care. I had already paid the legal fees of a courier of mine once, and he walked. Plus, I had more money than I had time to hide. I often found myself forgetting all the places I'd hidden cash. Going to do laundry and unexpectedly finding a million stashed in the dryer was not an uncommon occurrence. It wasn't a success, either. It was excess, and it was adding an unnecessary burden to my life, because every additional item I had bought had become one more thing to manage, store, repair, and move. I needed to get rid of things, not accumulate things. I needed to emulate the happiest people I knew—my longtime friends— who were living quietly. The ones who were thankful for what they had, and patient for what was to come.

BEFORE I HEADED TO CALI, it was late 2008, and I had a discreet personal obligation to attend to at Mom's house. And since she was away on vacation with Jim, I found myself standing alone in their backyard, with a present I wanted to bury for them in case I died first. Partly so Mom would be proud of me, and partly so she wouldn't need to complain about a lack of money ever again. The gift was a toolbox, filled with close to $2 million worth of gold bars. I figured it would be enough for Mom to relax and do what she loved most: camp in the Adirondacks and make pottery.

I wanted to bury the gold before the winter freeze, although the ground was already pretty stiff, but not too stiff. So I threw my scarf over my left shoulder, got down on one knee, and started banging through the thin frost line with a metal stake and a small sledgehammer.

Once I broke through to warmer soil, I reached for my shovel and started digging and digging. The deeper the hole became, the more I could feel the electron flow of the earth calming me. I think it was the grounding energy I was missing, and probably why the Mandarin Oriental could charge me $500 for a hot stone massage.

After my shovel was a little over three feet deep in the ground, next to the house foundation, sweat began forming around my hairline. There was a part of me that wanted to sit in the hole and relax, but it was time to lower the one-hundred-pound box of gold bars slowly into the hole with straps, the same way a coffin is lowered.

Mom, I know we all make mistakes, but I hope this helps, I thought, hovering over the hole, with my deerskin gloves on, straps wrapped tight around my hands. The toolbox felt heavier than it was, and after I carefully positioned it deep in the earth, I let it go. I then began meticulously backfilling it with sand and stones.

I was only twenty-nine, but if I was on my deathbed before Mom, I could hopefully whisper in her ear, "At the back left corner of your house, dig down three feet next to the foundation. I left a present for you. I love you."

I don't think I'd ever said "I love you" to Mom in a meaningful way, without a quiver in my chest. I had signed birthday cards with, "Love, Eric," and said, "I luv you" so fast it was almost one syllable—without depth. But saying it and actually feeling it . . . that never happened. I only felt it when I said it to our family dog, Franny. I really loved that pooch. No matter how bad shit was, that bird dog always wagged her tail and nuzzled up to me. Even when I said "I love you" to Jill, I don't think I completely felt it, because I'd built up a really strong wall around my heart.

I think it took me a long time to notice the wall, because I created a whirlwind existence by living with a can-do-every-thing-in-life mentality. I was always looking for the next deal, the next dollar, and the next rush. It's how I equated my worth. I equated it by *how much* I was doing, rather than by *what* I was doing. And the faster I moved, the less I felt. I was always *busy, busy, busy.* I think subconsciously I was just waiting for the right woman to say, "Good job, Eric. You did it. We don't need anything else. I'll still love you, even if we can't afford to keep up with the newest trends."

18

SPREAD THIN

I had just landed in Northern California. Every time I was there, it felt like I was at the forefront of new ways of doing business. There were so many dreamers and innovative thinkers in the region. The veneer of fear, insecurity, and self-consciousness that permeated the East Coast wasn't as noticeable there. The rural communities focused on creativity, awareness, and sustainability. They also focused on the state's largest cash crop: Sweet Mary Jane. Especially in The Emerald Triangle, which is about four hours north of San Francisco. It grows some of the best outdoor weed in the world, thanks to the area's rich soil and Mediterranean climate.

I had several weed connections in the area, but I only had a history of working with one. Her name was Cora, and she was tall, strong, down to earth, and serious. Most importantly, she was a retired weed broker and expat who had lived in Central America for several years but still collected commissions on the beach when I periodically shipped weed to one of her past customers in Atlanta, or when one of her past connections occasionally supplied me. However, after she'd recently been robbed at gunpoint in Central America, she decided to move back to

California and jump back into the weed game. In a way, we were brokers for each other, but she didn't have much working capital, so we often used my money to grease the wheels.

"THERE'S A SLIGHT DELAY," Cora said, standing with me at a gas station in a remote Northern town in Cali. "The order I'd reserved for you has been sold, but I have other good things in the works."

"How good of things?" I asked in dismay. "I just paid twenty grand to get my crew and cash here for *that* order."

"The quality is phenomenal, but it costs more than what I originally said."

Are you fucking kidding me? I thought. Before I flew there, I explicitly told Cora not to waste my time—after she'd recently delivered me some outdoor weed that she'd reassured me was indoor weed. She'd tried to trick me, not thinking I'd know the difference. But after I complained for about an hour, she broke down and lowered the price with a guarantee she wouldn't bait-and-switch me again. The discount helped, although now I was stuck in Cali with $1.5 million in my rental car, Missy en route to pick up the weed, and Rob—whom I flew in for training—on standby in a hotel. So my only logical choice was to accept whatever Cora was going to piecemeal.

"How long is this gonna take?" I asked, knowing I had to get back to Saratoga for Canadian deliveries that were waiting to be received, graded, sorted, and distributed.

"Not more than a day or two," she answered, unconvincingly.

Cora knew a lot of people in the weed game, but many of them were flakes. I admired her hustle, but disliked her trying to make a quick buck at my expense. She threw too many things at the wall, hoping something would stick, and at times, I thought she was jealous of me because I was younger and made more money. I hated that feeling, because what she didn't understand was that my rewards came from the things I did constantly, not on occasion. I didn't just dip into the game and try to make a quick million. No, my millions came from the experience of thousands and thousands of deals, through both the floods and the droughts.

Cora was in her late thirties, and even though she rejected social norms and lived nonviolently outside the law, I didn't consider her a hippy. Instead, I considered her a business-woman, but lately she'd been troublesome. She was manipu-lating facts to make *her* life easier, not mine. I'll admit, though, I've shaded the truth to be a productive member of society. I've also tried to justify my little white lies by telling myself, "Everyone else is lying, so I might as well, too." Or, "I wasn't lying; I was just shading the truth." Regardless of my excuses, whenever I caught someone lying, I saw two options: continue the relationship or end it. And since neither Cora nor I were Pinocchio, we pushed forward with one common goal: make more money, then use that money to make more money.

Cora escorted me, my cash, and Rob to her associates' small cabin in the Redwood Forest. We sat there for four days with spotty cell service while Cora tried to fill my order. Most of the growers she'd lined up to show their harvests didn't show up on time, and some didn't show up at all. It was sloppy business, and I was breaking my own rules by meeting several new faces. Eventually, I told Cora I'd wait in the basement when the growers stopped by, in order to maintain anonymity. I told her she could bring the samples down to me, alone, for my inspec-tion and approval.

It made me nervous how all the growers had such go-with-the-flow attitudes. They didn't understand the game. None of them understood how the DEA builds cases using parallel construction, which is a common method used by law enforce-

ment to build separate sources of evidence around an individual, in order to conceal how the original evidence was found. It's
a strategy that protects the identity of thousands of unknown
government informants, who are currently dispersed among
every town and city in the nation. These informants are good at
blending in. They're white-collar, blue-collar, and gangster.
They always have a cover story, and that's why it's hard to know
who to trust in the underworld. It's also why I needed to have
good intuition. I had to be able to know without knowing—
which was about living a life based on gut feelings, ones that
definitely saved me from countless disasters.

While Cora gradually filled my order, Missy patiently waited
for three nights at a nearby hotel and I taught Rob how to grade,
buy, package, and conceal weed in wooden shipping crates. By
day four, the order was filled and Missy came to the cabin to
load her cargo trailer. I was livid when I noticed she didn't have
any professional logos on the trailer as I had instructed. She had
simply taped an 8.5" x 11" piece of paper to the back door. It
looked like something she'd printed on a tiny home printer,
which was low on ink. The paper was already close to falling off,
and would surely disintegrate with the first drop of rain. I didn't
think the deal could get any more sour.

"What the fuck is she doing?" I asked Rob, who was standing
next to me on the outside deck of the cabin.

I could see Cora and Missy talking at the end of the dirt
driveway, sharing a joint, which was a huge no-no.

"I think Missy has some weed stashed in her driver's side
door," Rob replied, quietly.

I couldn't believe it. Missy was there to hitch up her discred-
itable trailer and leave, but now Cora was cozying up to her—
probably to use Missy's transport services in the future, behind
my back, for other deals. I presumed Cora's motive, because
she'd asked me several times in the days prior if she could use

Missy to bring one of her weed orders back East, along with mine. But I said "no" because I didn't want Missy making extra stops or co-mingling with another crew that could possibly expose my operation to law enforcement. It's also why Missy shouldn't have seen Cora's face. Because keeping all arms of my organization separate is how I maintained a low profile. It's also how I had stayed off the DEA's radar for a record number of years.

As I walked down the dusty driveway toward Missy and Cora, I calmed myself before saying, "Please don't smoke near the cab of the truck; you're going to stink it up."

I tried not to come across as a boss, but we'd just spent a dozen hours triple sealing close to five hundred individual pounds of weed that'd be undetectable by K-9s, and now smoke was drifting into the open doors of the dually's quad cab. *What a disgrace,* I thought.

As they both stepped back from the truck, Missy redirected her exhale into the sky, while passing the pipe to Cora for another drag.

When I looked down into the side pocket of the driver's side door, I saw a mangled sandwich baggie, which contained a handful of stinky weed. I also saw remnants of a broken-up bud on the driver's side floor mat. I was boiling inside, but I couldn't create any tension between us before Missy took off with my million-dollar load. El Chapo probably would've left them both there in the ditch, but I chose to bite my tongue as they continued smoking, watching me submissively shake out Missy's floor mat.

I felt disrespected. I had an urge to lash out, but I didn't, because like Jim often told me, "Eric, people who get offended are weak. No one wants to associate with weak people." He'd lay in more, saying my expectations were the root of all my problems, and that I should expect nothing from others in order to avoid disappointments in life. Mom would chime in with, "The world doesn't revolve around you, Eric. People are rude and disrespectful for the same reason they're polite and respectful—it comes down to the way they were raised. Someday you'll thank your mother."

19

INTERNAL CONFLICT

Five days later, Missy arrived safely with my load in Saratoga Springs, eagerly asking when she could do another run. So I had her do a few more runs, because I was able to negotiate favorable terms with other suppliers in The Emerald Triangle, and confirm that California was a long-term viable weed source. However, on Missy's third run I noticed she'd broken into one of my wooden crates and stolen some weed to smoke on the drive. She'd then tried to reseal the package of weed and renail the crate closed, thinking I wouldn't notice. When I questioned her, her claim was, "My dirt bike peg poked a hole in the crate, and I tried to fix it."

I was fuming. I don't think Missy knew lying is how people usually get hurt in the underworld, but luckily for her, I wasn't the type of guy to give her a lesson. Instead, I started shuffling in one of my other East Coast drivers to temporarily make the Cali runs, while I solidified plans to use a private jet to transport cash to the West Coast, and a trucking company to bring weed to the East Coast.

I had four custom road cases manufactured to transport cash. Each case had wheels for easy transport, and could hold $1 million in twenties. On the tarmac, the cases would appear to contain film equipment, and once my cash arrived safely in Cali, I'd mix weed with legitimate produce in a tractor-trailer. It was the safest way to move large volumes of weed cross country, because California is the largest producer of fruits and vegetables in the nation. Plus, police rarely search tractor-trailers unless they get a tip, or the driver's log records are inadequate at checkpoints.

IT WAS ALMOST summer and I was at the Bonnaroo Music Festival on a farm in Tennessee, bobbing my head to David Byrne as he performed, "Once in a Lifetime."

I heard a burner ring in my pocket. It was Rob.

"Yo, what's up!" I shouted, pressing the phone tight to my right ear while plugging my left to hear.

"The trailer's loaded, but I couldn't fill the entire order. I'm finding that it dries up around here in the summer. I could only get three hundred units and I don't want to fill the rest with left-over trash," Rob replied, from our house in Cali, which we'd recently leased for our West Coast headquarters. "Also, Missy's a mess. She doesn't want me to escort her to the highway."

I had trained Rob for the last six months so he could manage my Cali operation on his own, and against my better judgment, I'd slid Missy back in the queue to do one last run because she had an outstanding balance of $300,000 with me for a Canadian load I'd sold her the prior week. I assumed a Cali run would reduce her balance, before she smoked the profits.

"Put her on the phone," I replied.

"Hey, sweetie," Missy said.

"Listen, he's just going to follow you to the on-ramp, to act as a decoy, in case there are any cops around," I said with sympathy and care, yet secretly wanting to throw her into the lions' den.

"I gotchu, baby. I'll see you in five days," she replied in her crowd-pleasing tone.

I snapped the phone shut with one hand, realizing what a mess my operation had become, but I didn't want to think about it because I was on vacation. Plus, Rob was trustworthy and had successfully completed his first deal on his own. And Missy was on the road now, so I tried not to worry about her as I slipped back into the music—whispering "Once in a Lifetime" lyrics into the crowd, as three grams of mushrooms started to flood my bloodstream and loosen my jaw.

I was attending Bonnaroo with a couple of lifetime friends and a girl I'd met earlier in the year at the Coachella Valley Music and Arts Festival. Part of me regretted being at Bonnaroo, because I barely knew the girl and Rob could've used my help in Cali. But I was trying to break my escort habit by seeing if I could open my heart, instead of my wallet. Plus, Ava's phone number had faded away in my jeans' pocket while in the washing machine, so that dream was kissed goodbye the first and last night I saw her. I couldn't find Summer's phone number online either, probably because she regularly changed her Eros profile to evade law enforcement.

Fuck yeah! The shrooms were working. I felt like I was floating. I could still feel the beer cans that were scattered amongst the field, crushing under my feet, but they felt soft and I felt weightless. That's when I began to sing along with the crowd: *"Into the blue again, after the money's gone!"*

I continued rambling on, rubbing shoulders with everyone around me as we melted into one. It felt like a communal experience. I could see and hear what others around me were thinking. We all appreciated the music, and that's when I remembered that tripping to live music was one of my favorite pastimes. I think it was the movement. Dancing shook off my pain and brought my body into balance, just like Jim often said: "Shake it off."

As soon as the encore started with "Burning Down the House," I was completely lit. *"Hold on tight, we're in for nasty weather . . . burning down the house!"* roared through the field, from the main stage, as I jumped for the stars, three heads above the crowd, ready to start a new life. I was ready to burn my house, watch it smolder, and rebuild it from the ash.

As I slipped deeper into thought, crystallized images of how beautiful life could become in the near future popped into my brain. I felt alive, unstoppable, and dangerous—not to society, but to myself. Soon I'd be in a position to do whatever I wanted in life. The days of hiding in the underworld and living a low profile were almost over. I could smell retirement in Hollywood around the corner.

I know I was cocky at Bonnaroo, because I was at a point in life where I had lost perspective of everything. The reality was, my business was *crumbling* and I was crumbling with it. But I tried to convince myself otherwise, even though deep down I was just a weak boy masking my insecurities with a big grin. Sure, all the ads for the festival portrayed it as a celebration, but I had nothing to celebrate, because I was lost and I was torn. I didn't want to give up my empire. It was my baby. I'd started it from nothing, and now I was distraught because there was no more room to grow it. At least, not without a gun.

I had maxed out. My sales were slumping, America was becoming flooded with weed, and people like Missy needed to pay up and get kicked to the curb. The problem was, considering my level in the game now, the only way to successfully run the company would have been to enforce my rules and maintain my territory through violence, but I couldn't cross that line. It wasn't me. Therefore, my passion and dedication to my enterprise was fading and creating internal conflict that I couldn't exactly cry about to a psychotherapist. What would I say? "Hey, Doc, my business doesn't involve lawyers and signed agreements. Should I use a gun to enforce the rules?" I'm sure they would have 9-1-1 on the phone as soon as I stepped foot out of their office.

I was simply out of solutions, and my self-worth was diminishing fast. Why? Because my self-worth was based on my business and the money I had made. It was based on the value I had to offer the world, and my value was dealing. It was the main thing I was good at, and now with my identity at stake, my mind was overloaded with irrational thoughts. I wondered what my value to the world would be if I could no longer give people money or jobs. I wondered how much money my future wife would need to be happy. I wondered if I'd be able to buy my future kids what they needed. I didn't want to have a family that argued over finances. I didn't even know if Hollywood was a sure bet, or if I'd even like it. The only thing I knew was, I wasn't picking up a gun, and I was tired of operating under an alias, while taking thirty-plus phone calls a day in the underworld.

This left me with one option: I had to prepare for the unknown future. And the only way I knew how to prepare for the unknown was to bury $5 million worth of gold bars deep in the forest, miles from the stash I'd buried for Mom. And that's exactly what I did, buried gold—in hopes it'd save me from my reality—one I'd spent years building, and one I couldn't imagine my life would become without. It was a reality I had desperately tried to patch up for as long as possible, no matter how exhausting or painful the process became. It was a reality that was difficult to make a clean break from, because I was resisting the only constant in life: change.

20

LOYALTY AND INTEGRITY

I t was June 16, 2009, and I'd just returned home from Bonnaroo, still feeling the clairvoyance of the mushrooms swirling through me. I had to take delivery of $4 million worth of weed between Missy and three of my Canadian suppliers. I also had a backlog of customers waiting on their orders, since I'd been out of town for over a week.

Missy was first up, because she'd already been waiting a couple hours at a nearby hotel for my arrival back into town. She was earlier than planned, which told me she'd broken the rules and had driven at night. I didn't care, though, because this was the last Cali run she was doing.

As I entered the mall parking lot to meet Missy, it was high noon and sunny. Our procedure was always the same: meet in a public parking lot, make eye contact, then she'd follow me to a random secluded place to unload her vehicle. This allowed me to confirm no one had been following her vehicle, before unloading it.

The mall parking was relatively quiet, except for in the corner of the lot, where I could see Missy in a small Ford F-150 rental truck, towing a new, wider cargo trailer, with temporary plates. *Where the fuck was her usual truck and trailer?* I wondered, as anger flared through me. I knew there was no way this suspicious-looking rig had driven 2,500 miles without getting pulled over. My grip tightened on the steering wheel, and the closer I got, the worse it looked. There was too much weight on the tongue of the trailer, making the back of the truck ride low and the front high. It was obvious the enclosed car hauler was too big for the small pickup truck. The entire setup looked like an uninsured Craigslist landscaping company—trying to make a quick buck without finishing the last job they were paid for.

From my driver's seat, I scanned the vicinity for law enforcement among the scattered parked cars. Since I didn't see anything suspicious, I made eye contact with Missy and nodded for her to follow me. I felt exhausted from lack of sleep, and I was so pissed with the entire situation that I just wanted it to be over. So I took a shortcut and led her to my personal residence in a suburban neighborhood, with a quiet cul-de-sac, filled with trees and happy families.

As Missy backed her cargo trailer up to my three-bay garage, I stepped out of my truck to greet her, infuriated but pretending not to be.

"How was the drive?" I asked, all business, through Missy's open driver's side window.

"Smooth as always, Sweetie," Missy said, popping her door to step out of the truck.

Missy had on a fresh-pressed, pink collared button-down, covering her inked-up arms. She looked well-rested and professional, almost too good for being on the road for four days.

As I circled Missy's trailer a couple times, something didn't feel right. Actually, there was always something that didn't feel right around her, but my greed kept me working with her, and with that greed came foolishness—because no matter how much money I had, it was never enough.

Missy could see my frustration and began explaining she'd bought the larger trailer last minute, because the new wooden crates I had custom built for her didn't fit into the old trailer by two inches, even though I had specifically called her for exact dimensions no fewer than three separate times. I'd even specified I didn't want the width of the trailer, just the width of the door opening. I then rounded down six inches from the number she gave me, to account for her brain fog.

While Missy continued rambling on, the sun dipped behind the clouds, the sky darkened, and I immediately saw a flash, just over her left shoulder, past my well-manicured yard. It was the daytime running lights of a tan, late-model Chevy Malibu, off in the distance. I assumed a sensor must have popped on automatically. The car was parked about two hundred yards away, in my neighbor's circular driveway. Right then, I knew we were followed.

"What the fuck is going on?" I whispered to Missy, through gritted teeth, staring directly at her, making sure not to look at what I suspected was an unmarked government car. "Don't fuck with me right now! Are you sure you drove this truck yourself?"

"Yeah, why? What's up?" she asked, her face filled with mock concern.

I wanted to wipe the sugary smile off her face, but instead, I signaled for her to follow me inside.

Our footsteps echoed throughout my unfurnished house, as she followed me up the stairs, past five empty bedrooms, to the one with a view of the neighbor's driveway. As sunlight filtered through the bedroom blinds, I turned to her, holding my index finger to my lips, signaling for her not to say a word, but to unbutton her shirt and prove she wasn't wearing a wire. She then immediately opened her shirt and I patted down her pockets. She was clean, but I took her burner and put it outside the bedroom door, in case it was bugged.

"Are you sure you drove this load yourself? This isn't a time for bullshit. That car followed you here!" I said, pointing through the crack in the blinds, showing her the car.

"Yeah, I drove the entire way myself!"

A contraction in her neck told me she was lying, but there was no time to argue. I had bigger problems.

My brain started grinding for an alibi. I figured I needed to unload at least one of her bikes. That would explain to the jury why she was at my house; she was there to leave a bike with me for our upcoming film shoot. For our web series. As far as what was in the wood crates: "I'm not sure—that's not my business, Your Honor."

"We have to go back outside, but make sure you don't look at that car. I don't want them to know we've noticed them," I said.

When we were back in the driveway, I pulled the trailer ramp down, stepped inside, and scanned the interior. I noticed a few of the screw heads in the wooden crates had been marred, so there was no question they'd been tampered with. Next, I allowed my eyes to travel slowly along the roof of the trailer, and then I saw what I was looking for. A GPS tracker, with a black wire exposed, where the wall met the ceiling. With closer inspection, I could see a large black battery pack and transmitter attached, stuffed behind the wall paneling.

My body tightened. This was it. After years of waiting, the day had finally arrived. It felt surreal. I think my body went numb for a second, as I looked over to Missy saying: "That's just the brake line, sweetie . . . or maybe it's for the lights."

I grinned and held my index finger to my lips, signaling her not to talk, in case audio was being transmitted from the trailer. Missy didn't understand what was going on, but I knew every move we made from here out was crucial. It was game time, and I wasn't giving up until they had us.

Stepping out of the trailer and into my garage, I tried to

enlighten Missy. "That's not a fucking brake line. It's a tracking device. Help me unload your dirt bike," I said, as she reached for her phone and proceeded to call the trailer manufacturer to ask if there were brake lines in the ceilings of their trailers.

I couldn't believe it; Missy still thought it was a brake line. Part of me wanted her to walk over to the cop's car so she could confess about all the idiotic choices she'd been making, and that she was finally ready to self-surrender.

After I wheeled Missy's dirt bike into my garage and securely locked the trailer back up, I told her to follow me in my truck. I figured by leaving with her, I'd be able to determine how big an investigation this was by how many vehicles were following us. Once I knew, I could decide where to leave the trailer. I also reminded Missy, if we were to get pulled over and separated, to keep her mouth shut until she had a lawyer, and she replied, "Relax, I know the rules."

I got in my truck and reversed down the narrow driveway, casually rolling out of my dog-friendly neighborhood as if I didn't have a care in the world. I made sure to keep my eyes off the unmarked car in the process.

Within a mile of my house, we passed over six unmarked cars, stuffed with government agents, tucked off the side of the road. My phone soon chirped through my pocket, and I answered.

"You're right, they're everywhere," Missy said, with fear in her voice.

"Yeah, I'm sorry to say, I think there are too many clouds for us to film today," I replied, assuming her burner was tapped.

I clenched my jaw. I suspected she'd lied about driving the load herself, and I was pissed, because her scam had just cost me a $1.1 million load.

"I got this," she replied, before I heard the silence of our disconnected call.

As I stayed within the speed limit, I saw no one following behind, but I could hear the distant hum of an engine and immediately saw a small prop plane circling above. My blood started pumping. There was no doubt, some task force thought I was important.

At the next stop sign, I switched back into defense mode with laser-like focus. I then took a casual left turn and split off from Missy. After a mile or so, I realized the plane followed her and the tracking device, and since I was now out of sight, I floored it toward the outskirts of town, because I needed to escape without looking like I was trying to.

As I drove the curvy backroads, I took five of my burners out of the center console and snapped each in half, one by one. I then took out the batteries, looked in my rearview again, and still didn't see any tails. So I slowed down to about forty miles per hour, and I started flinging individual parts of the phones out my passenger window into a gully of tall grass and uninhabited woods. I made sure the parts were far enough apart, to prevent them from ever being found, reassembled, and investigated. The last piece of evidence was my accounts receivable ledger, on a small piece of paper, folded up in my wallet. I tried to memorize the encoded list, before tearing it into tiny pieces and sending it out the window like snowflakes in the wind.

I picked up speed, redlining my engine out of every corner into the straights. Big Rig was working hard, rapidly shifting gears. My brain was working hard, too, as the warm summer wind blew through the cab, pushing my hair sideways. I took a moment to enjoy the fresh air, knowing summer, my favorite season in Saratoga, was about to be taken from me. And Mom was right again . . . "You better appreciate what you have, because soon it will turn into what you had."

Eventually, I neared town and hit a red light. While waiting, I kept an eye on my mirror and soon spotted two of the unmarked cars rolling up about four cars back. I stayed calm. I needed help. I needed help from someone I could trust. Someone who was consistent. Someone who supported me, even when they didn't need anything from me. It was time to pull my safety valve: Jim.

Jim was the stepfather who was always there for me in emergencies. He had raced me to the hospital through red lights several times as a kid for stitches. He was also there for me as a young adult when I was airlifted to the hospital twice. Once when I lit myself on fire while using gasoline to light a brush pile, and a second time when I hit a tree skiing, broke eleven ribs, and collapsed a lung. And like clockwork, Jim was always the first person to drop what he was doing and arrive on scene ready to assist in any manner possible. Even though we weren't close, he helped me and I helped him. Mostly when I fed him and Mom with my water feature proceeds, after he had lost his job in the 2001 recession. It felt good to help them until Jim landed his new job several years later. Partly, because I like to help others, but also because it was my form of saying, "You see, I told you I'd make it on my own."

Yeah, of course I had something to prove to Mom and Jim, because when someone beats you down, by default you're going to want to show them your eventual success. Just listen to Tupac. I listen to him and Nipsey whenever I need some inspiration. They understood pain. Regardless, Jim never failed me and he stood behind his vows to Mom, too. He was loyal, and that loyalty combined with his integrity put him at the top of my list in any emergency.

"Where are you? I need to see you. It's an emergency!" I shouted to Jim, through my personal iPhone, the only phone I hadn't chucked out the window.

"I'm at work. What's wrong?"

"It's too complicated to discuss on the phone. I'll come see you. I'll be at your office in thirty minutes."

"Okay, but meet me at the gas station across the street," Jim said.

Jim had recently started working again, this time as a customer service manager in the renewable energy industry. His office was near Albany, New York, about a half-hour drive south from where I was aimlessly driving. I hoped to make it there without getting pulled over.

When I merged onto the triple-lane highway, I drove casually with the traffic and watched for the two distant, unmarked Fed cars in my rearview. My heart was pounding. I had to force myself to breathe. I want to say I couldn't believe it, but I could . . . my entire life had changed in an instant. It was no longer about the next deal; it was now about simple things, like being thankful for sunlight. Fuck, I didn't want to go to jail.

After ten minutes of cruising, I assumed the Feds had run my license plate, and probably had GPS tracking my iPhone or Onstar, but I still wanted to try to lose them, so I maintained a little over sixty-five miles per hour in the left passing lane, with two semi-trucks to my right, letting the traffic build up behind us. And once there was a clusterfuck of cars behind me, I inched ahead of the semis and switched into the right lane in front of them—out of the Feds' sight. I then punched it, and within seconds Big Rig was doing one hundred miles per hour. I felt like I'd just gotten my first sucker punch in, because I knew it would've taken a solid three minutes for the congestion I'd created to loosen up and for them to realize I was gone.

A couple minutes later, I sharply exited the highway and the Feds were nowhere to be seen, and when I finally made it to the gas station, I pulled in, to the sight of Jim standing tall in a gray suit, next to his car, coffee in hand.

"Listen, I only have a few seconds to talk. I'm going to get arrested any minute," I said frantically, wishing Jim could rush me offshore as quickly as he'd rushed me to emergency rooms.

"What are you talking about?" Jim asked.

"Please, I need you to listen very carefully," I said, each word deliberate. "In your basement, in the bottom of Grandma's old picnic basket, there's a quarter-million dollars hidden. Please use it to retain the best criminal attorney possible. Call Lisa— she'll help you find one." Lisa was my corporate attorney, who knew nothing of my illicit endeavors.

I couldn't see Jim's eyes through his aviator sunglasses, so I wasn't sure if he was processing what I was saying.

"Slow down. Where'd you get that much cash and why's it in my house?" Jim asked, calmly sipping his coffee.

"I was in the wrong place at the wrong time. I can't explain now," I answered, scanning the area for unmarked cars. "I have to go. I'm trusting you with my life."

I wasn't sure if Jim was fazed by what I said, but I knew he wouldn't steal from me because he lived simply, like nature. He was calm, too. Probably because he was older now and knew how to think through problems before reacting to them. He knew life was no longer about what happened to him, but rather how he reacted to it. He was at the next level. At least I hoped so, because as he watched me coast off from the gas station, there was a slight part of me that wondered if he believed what I'd just told him.

I think it was my unhealed feelings toward Jim that still made me question him. I'd still get that little agitating twitch when I was near him, because the fact was, unless I was in critical condition, I was used to him saying, "Never cry wolf," which was frustrating, because even the main person I trusted, I still couldn't completely trust. But I was in a jam, and I had to believe he knew this was an emergency. This is when it really sank in. . . . I'm a criminal. I'm an outlaw. I break rules to get ahead. Who will be there for me when I stand before the judge? I knew who: my money.

As I drove off without a destination, my heart rate was still up, and I considered my two options. One, I could drive back home and get arrested. Two, I could ditch my phone and truck, never contact anyone from my past again, and immediately hail a cab to an associate to get a passport to the tune of about sixty grand. Option two meant leaving the country as a fugitive, which was a tough idea to swallow. That left me with option one, which was okay because I had prepared for this war for years, despite not knowing what the exact scenario would be. I only knew it would cost a lot of cash, which I had safely stashed. I also knew Jim always said, "Don't start a job you can't finish," and I knew this was a venture that if left abandoned would haunt me for the rest of my life—even if I created the best false trails possible.

I twistedly liked the idea of playing "catch me if you can . . . I'm the Gingerbread Man," but it wouldn't have been sustainable. Yeah, I could've disappeared with a lot of money, but I had bigger dreams that money and seclusion couldn't fulfill. I wanted to help the world with a legitimate enterprise. I wanted to make a positive impact. I wanted to say, "Mom, look, I did it! You can stop worrying."

I deduced there was only one way to finish this. I had to drive back to my house in Saratoga and face the law, which was a depressing thought, but my hope was the arrest would go smoothly.

As I maintained the speed limit home, I had my seat belt on, and my hands at ten and two on the wheel, just like I was taught in Driver's Ed. For some odd reason, I thought if I looked like a model citizen they'd go easier on me. Like maybe they'd think I was a good kid in the wrong place at the wrong time.

With my windows still down, I took in as much fresh air as

possible and slipped into tunnel vision. I could see the broken white lines that divided the lanes in front of me turn into solid white lines, and with that, my distress turned to anger. There was a primal part of me that wanted to know who the fuck had my trailer of weed and what it was going to take to get it back. I didn't like losses, and with this loss, I instantly felt all of Missy's lies at once, and I wanted to make her pay. Immediately.

I WAS ONLY a mile from my house when I decided to stop and fill my gas tank. I wanted any advantage I could get in the situation, and right then having a full tank before I confronted the enemy felt safer than arriving with half a tank. To me, it was about preparing for the worst, like I always had, ever since Mom looked down at me and said, "You'll have no place to live, if ever you do that again." But no matter how much I prepared in life, there were still times when I fell. Especially when I exited the convenience store after paying the cashier for my gas.

"Down on the ground! Down on the ground! Down on the ground!" I heard screamed, accompanied by stomping footsteps rushing in from behind me.

I quickly dropped to my knees, then to my chest. I wasn't expecting the ambush.

"Hands where I can see them! Don't move!" I heard.

With my face on the oil-stained pavement, I spread my legs and arms. My body twitched; I hadn't been pinned down like that since I was fed dish soap. I didn't say a word.

I was quickly patted down, my keys and wallet were taken from my pocket, and cuffs were cinched around my bony wrists. I was then immediately stuffed into the front passenger seat of an unmarked Chevy Suburban. The entire extraction took seconds, and the onlookers were clueless because they didn't see any government uniforms. It looked like I was being kidnapped.

It was just two regular-looking guys, with their DEA badges discreetly clipped to their belts and hidden by their untucked T-shirts. Although, I did see a backup, local, marked police car in the distance, in the adjacent parking lot. I assumed it was on standby, in case I decided to run.

One agent drove me in a Suburban to my home and the other followed us, driving my truck.

"What's your name, kid?" the agent driving me asked.

Right then, I knew the enemy knew nothing about me. Not even my fucking name! Are you kidding me? *Thank you, universe!* I thought. My day had just gotten a whole lot better, and I remained calm, knowing the DEA doesn't waste time, money, and resources chasing unknown targets. They do their homework first. I was just a bystander in a case I knew nothing about yet.

"Eric," I replied. "I'm confused, sir. Can you please tell me what's going on?"

I didn't want to request an attorney yet. I wanted to befriend him first, to gain as much information as possible about the case. And in order to do so, I needed him to think there was a chance I'd cooperate with him.

"Well, Eric, I'm here to help you, but your window of opportunity is limited. I can tell you from experience that if you help us, your life will be a whole lot easier," he answered, his head cocked toward me before looking back at the road.

"I want to help. Just tell me what's going on," I repeated, hoping to crack him.

"There's a lot of marijuana in that trailer, and I know you know something about it."

I now assumed the trailer had been pulled over and searched for a traffic violation somewhere between California and Saratoga. It seemed like a short and fast-paced investigation, and they were seeking clues in any way possible. This might just be my lucky day, I thought, because I still hadn't been caught breaking the law. I never unloaded the weed from the trailer, so my hands were clean, as of now.

"I'm sorry, I'm very confused. I'd like to speak with my lawyer, please," I replied, leaning back further into the seat, hands cuffed behind me.

I was done talking and ready to watch things play out. I wanted them to draw their own conclusions. It didn't matter whether I was breaking the law or not. It was time to remain silent.

HOLY FUCK! It was a zoo when we pulled up to my house. There were over ten unmarked DEA cars, two state trooper cars, and Missy's truck and trailer. There were also a few curious neighbors in the street, who would surely no longer recognize me as the quiet guy with the neighborly wave. I saw Missy being interrogated in the back seat of a car, and prayed she'd avoid running her mouth for once. If she kept it shut, we could beat this because none of our fingerprints were on the packaged weed, and the Feds couldn't prove who had loaded the merchandise onto the trailer. I'd set up the transportation in a manner that meant we could claim plausible deniability in a court of law. I had planned for this. It's why I had the weed packaged professionally and sealed in wooden crates by Rob, who used rubber gloves, so the load couldn't be connected to him, either. The DEA had nothing, except three giant sealed crates of weed that a jury couldn't attach to anyone. Case dismissed.

The DEA agents walked me around to my backyard, where about fifteen other agents were standing and wondering what was inside my house. The sun was beating down on all of us, and as I leaned against the steel, vertical bar fencing surrounding my pool, I tried to figure out who the boss was. I was left clueless, though.

"Is this your house?" a flustered agent asked me, his cell phone glued to his right ear, waiting for confirmation on a search warrant.

"Yeah," I answered, wanting to knock the phone out of his hand and school him on probable cause. I could tell these guys didn't play by the rules, because they didn't have one valid reason to enter my house.

"Do we have permission to go inside?" he asked, pacing, waiting on his phone.

"No," I replied.

He shot me a fiery look, switching his focus back to his phone call, determined to get inside my home one way or another.

My anger quickly turned back to fear, and my throat swelled. I had enough incriminating evidence in my house to be hung without trial. "Can I please call my lawyer?" I requested, but he blew me off, pretending not to hear.

I was on my own. The only thing I could do was listen, think, and control how I responded.

BY MID-AFTERNOON it was in the high eighties, and I was still cuffed and standing near the pool when the next agent approached me. It was the first time I'd seen his face, because he'd been busy grilling Missy in his Chevy Malibu, parked in my driveway. He was the most relaxed of the bunch, notepad in hand, pressed jeans, white polo shirt, and shiny white New Balance sneakers with a few grass stains. He was young, less than ten years my senior. I was surprised when he read my Miranda warning off a small card in his wallet. He was the first agent to comply with my constitutional rights. It seemed he was by the book, and I could tell he wanted a promotion at my expense.

"What's your name?" he asked calmly, sweat dripping down his face.

"Eric," I answered, hoping Missy hadn't flipped to Team USA yet.

"Well, Eric, we have a search warrant on the way, but before it shows up you can help yourself. Is there anything you want to tell me?"

"Yes, I want to call my lawyer, please. My phone is in my truck," I replied, trying to sense if he was bluffing about the warrant, but his humble attitude left me clueless.

The agent informed me his name was Special Agent Ron Arp, with the DEA Task Force, and I assumed he was the boss, because his notepad and pen were much more intimidating than his badge and gun. He looked like a soft intern taking notes. He was calm. He was a listener and a thinker. He was an observer, and quite similar to me, because we were both using patience to gain deeper insight into our predicament. It was the type of patience very few people possess, but the ones who do are usually the most successful. They're confident, and they'll painstakingly wait for anything just to get what they want. I could only hope I was more patient than Ron, because if he lost his patience first, I'd surely win this battle.

EVENTUALLY, one of the agents allowed me to use his phone to call my attorney, Lisa, and when she answered, I quickly explained I was under arrest, agents were trying to search my house, and that I needed assistance. I got as far as "Please come to 22 Preserve Way—" when the agent yanked the phone from my handcuffed hands.

"No, she's not allowed here!" he yelled, cutting me off.

I instantly felt my rights being violated, and that's when I remembered why I broke the law. It was because I felt I had an unfair start among my peers, but I knew that'd be a hard sell to any federal judge now.

After the agent cut my lifeline, the entire circus continued waiting feverishly around my house like Black Friday shoppers outside Target, and by 4 p.m. they started to look lethargic and I became optimistic. I started to think maybe they wouldn't be granted a bogus search warrant, but I thought too soon, because a few moments later an electric current ran through the crowd and the agents began snapping on blue rubber gloves.

STILL STANDING NEAR MY POOL, I immediately became furious as I watched them use my keys to open the side door to my house, and swarm into it like it was their first Easter egg hunt.

I couldn't believe it. The agents had gone rogue. They somehow finagled to get a search warrant, even though they didn't have probable cause to be in my home. What they had was the training and resources to do their job legally, but they were cheating the system for a quick win—just like I had. Too bad we weren't friends. We could've all been rich.

"Holy shit! There's so much cash, I can barely pick it up," an agent shouted in victory from my garage door to the agents outside. "The bag must weigh over a hundred pounds!"

I saw that coming. They would've had to have been twelve blind mice not to find my cash.

"Bring 'em in," Ron smirked with a hand signal, motioning to the officer guarding me.

Ron sat me down at the kitchen table, which had $1.5 million in cash sitting on top of it. It was recovered from a duffel bag in the hallway closet. Ron made sure I was sitting close enough to practically rub my nose in it. I felt helpless. I wanted revenge. They'd just taken my money illegally.

Ron continued to remain quiet and humble. I could tell he wasn't a talker; he was a doer—and he wanted answers. I could see the determination in his face for *more*. More cash, more information, and more busts . . . anything to boost his career.

The cash was ready for one of my Canadian suppliers, arriving with a load later that evening at a nearby truck stop. The supplier was just waiting on a text confirmation from me, with the exact meeting time. I could hear and see his burner among others on my kitchen counter—alerting me with new text messages every minute. Ron noticed the flashing red lights too. "There are a lot of people trying to get a hold of you right now," he said. "This is your one opportunity to work with me. If you do, you don't have to go to jail. I'll make things easy for you. No one has to know about this," he pitched, in his final attempt to get me to join Team USA.

There were eleven burners laid out on the kitchen counter and Ron wanted me to conduct business as usual, with him secretly in the background building cases. The thought disgusted me. I'd rather die. I could only hope he wouldn't pretend to be me and use my phones to set up my associates.

I didn't say a word to Ron. I didn't even say "no." I was so fucking pissed with Missy. . . . Between the weed seized in her trailer, the cash in my house, and what she still owed, I had already lost three million that afternoon and I didn't know what Ron would go after next. I could deal with the fact he had me cuffed, but the fact that he had just taken my money with a faulty warrant was burning me up. It was unjust and part of me wanted to snap, but I had to stay clear-headed to keep my organization safe.

As I remained cuffed at the table among the agents, I watched them bag up my cash, phones, and PGP Encrypted

Blackberries. Ron asked me to sign the large clear plastic evidence bags, but I didn't respond or sign anything. He was a confirmed enemy, and I looked like a fucking hostage sitting at the table with my hands cuffed behind my back as they continued waiting, hoping to crack me. I wanted to tell them they had nothing on me, but I wasn't about to let my emotions overpower my mission.

WITHIN TWENTY MINUTES, the agents started itching for dinner and one yelled out, "Who wants pizza?"

They were all for it, and simultaneously started searching their pockets for spare cash to throw into the pot.

I had an itch to show off, so I eventually broke my silence and said "I'll buy," with a grin, giving them two non-incriminating words for the record.

They all looked toward me, with my bagged-up cash in front of me, and laughed.

I wanted to leave them with one good laugh before we went to war, hoping I'd be the one laughing after winning in the courtroom. I wanted them to know this wasn't my first jam and that I'd get them back soon. Of course, I knew I had nothing to gain from my comment—it was just my weak method of collecting their attention, to recharge myself from their heyday. And I know Jim would've surely said, "You talk too much, Eric . . . never celebrate your win before you win." But no matter how many reminders Jim gave me, my unchecked ego had always been my most self-destructive flaw.

21

TRAPPED

Albany County Jail was a dump. A big box of concrete and steel, housing a bunch of inmates in yellow jumpsuits and orange slip-on shoes. You could probably buy the entire costume from China for ninety-nine cents. My mugshot, strip search, and fingerprinting happened during my check-in around 9 p.m.—according to the wall clock— which was the last thing I saw before a corrections officer escorted me to my accommodations: a six-by-eight-foot dirty cell with a steel toilet, steel sink, steel bed, and vinyl flame-resis- tant mattress that looked like it'd been through two life sentences.

After the officer locked me in, he uncuffed my hands through the bars and left me with a bedroll consisting of a ratty military-style blanket and a stained, threadbare towel.

"Sir, can I please have some toilet paper?" I asked the officer, as he turned to walk away.

"You already have some," he said, pointing to the small amount remaining next to my dilapidated toilet.

"There's not much left."

"Yeah, be careful. The closer you get to the end of the roll, the faster it goes—just like life. You'll figure it out," he chuckled, walking off with the keys to my freedom jangling from his belt.

I could tell my MacGyver skills weren't going to get me out of this one, but it was a relief to finally get those cuffs off.

Like any good soldier, I wanted to use the downtime to recharge for the next attack, so I stuck my head under my push-button sink to fuel up on water, and then took a seat on my bed to get my bearings. It was noisy on my block. The cavernous space echoed every sound, from every cell. The inmates sounded like a bunch of monkeys trapped in a zoo, and amongst them, I eventually heard one, a few cells down, yell, "Yo, new guy, what are you in for?" But I blew him off, knowing any inmate could've been a government informant, because they're in every jail and in every prison. They're called snitches, and they'll do anything to save themselves.

WITHIN AN HOUR, the officer on patrol came around and switched off the fluorescent light in each of our cells, one by one. That's when I carefully took one piece of toilet paper, tore it in half, and wadded each piece into a ball so I could plug my ears against the clamor.

When I laid back on the concave mattress, I could hear and feel my heartbeat slow down from the intense day; the toilet paper muffled everything else around me. I must say, it was the first night in years I wasn't busy, and surprisingly, I wasn't stressed either, because I knew the government had a weak case. Plus, I had enough cash buried in the Adirondack Mountains to fight, but I still needed to make a legit phone call—which I still hadn't been granted. My only hope was that Jim and Lisa would soon figure out where I was and rescue me at a fair price.

As I laid there next to the concrete wall, I began to miss the safe harbor I usually retreated to after a hard day's work. It was that peaceful place next to a woman where I didn't have to pretend to be somebody I wasn't. It was the place where I felt loved. The place where I'd recharge and strengthen myself so I could go back out into the world and get everything I was told I couldn't have. But there was no space between me and that wall for a woman, because the steel bed was only thirty inches wide. It was also part of the reason I never got married, because I always knew you couldn't bring your wife to prison, and I subconsciously knew I'd be in jail one day. I just didn't know when, or for how long. I only knew being separated from a wife and kids would've been difficult, at least based on the women I'd dated, because I didn't think any of them could've handled separation. I would only have married a woman who could handle the ebbs and flows of life. One who understood how to take turns being strong for each other, when the other feels weak. Because in my opinion, that's what a strong relationship is about. It's about having two strong sides, like a bridge.

I WOKE the following morning to a guard passing me a tray of oatmeal, milk, and canned peaches through an opening in the steel bars. The peaches looked like leftovers from World War II.

On a positive note, that first night in jail was the best night's sleep I'd had in years. I slept eight hours straight, without turning once. I think it's because the event I'd feared for years had finally come . . . and I found peace in it. I'd been captured, and even though I couldn't predict my future, I couldn't see it getting much worse. Actually, there was some freedom in being locked in a cell. I felt unchained from my phones. The phones that owned me. Seriously, I didn't own them. They owned me, and I was tired of trying to satisfy everyone through them. I needed a retreat, and this one felt like my first vacation since I was sixteen, when I saw Dad on my last court-ordered visit.

After finishing my oatmeal, I bent over the sink, clasped one hand under the faucet, and splashed cold water on my face. I then raised my head to look in the scratched-up, eight-by-ten-inch non-breakable mirror, securely fastened to the wall. I couldn't see my face clearly, but I could see several large chunks of my life flashing before my eyes. Fuck, I was only thirty, and I looked toasted. I knew it was my lifestyle, because I had unconsciously created a hectic one, and along with that, everyone around me had become annoying. So much so, I'd become irritable at the slightest misunderstandings. But in this very moment, I could see that the problem wasn't with them—it was with me. I didn't know how to say "no." I just kept taking on more and more responsibilities while I chugged along, deteriorating from the inside out.

Yeah, I could have gone to a doctor and temporarily masked my problems with the newest pill, but I innately knew all I really wanted to do was consume less, work less, and be healthier. Fuck, I needed to get back to my roots. So before I towel dried my face, I looked deeper into the mirror and told myself it was just a matter of time before I'd die, and that it was time to go back to living a simple life, which wouldn't be a step backward, but rather a step forward.

THAT AFTERNOON, my cell door opened and I received permission to call Lisa from the payphone in the common area of my high-security unit. All of the outgoing calls were recorded, and in my case surely monitored for any clues Special Agent Ron Arp could use against me. I was surprisingly amped for this new high-stakes game of cat and mouse, and not having a wife or children to be responsible for mitigated any potential downside. I felt I was getting ready to star in an adventure movie without the slightest clue to its ending. I wondered if I could beat the odds, and before picking up the phone, I reminded myself to keep my personal life and my next move private. Revealing any type of information about myself that Ron could leverage to his advantage would only weaken me.

"Eric! Are you okay?" Lisa asked.

I was happy to hear her voice.

"Everything's fine here. Has my stepfather contacted you?" I asked calmly, keeping the conversation short and productive.

"Yes, he's aware of your arrest and he'll be at your bail hearing with me tomorrow."

I was relieved to verify Jim's reliability.

"Thank you, Lisa. I can't talk much now. I'll see you in court tomorrow."

I didn't leave a speck of information for Ron to pursue, and confirmation that Jim and Lisa had joined my team allowed me to redirect my thoughts toward other upcoming problems I'd be facing once I was out on bail. Particularly, how to retrieve cash I had scattered around the country, without Ron trailing me and dissecting my network one connection at a time. I knew he and his comrades would be on me like white on rice the minute I saw daylight. I also knew he wanted me out on bail—specifically so he could track me, get to know me, and build more cases. Therefore I needed to create a smokescreen, something to redirect his attention while I tied up the loose ends of my lawless lifestyle. There was no room for error. Ron had won the first battle, but I intended to win the war.

THE FOLLOWING DAY, my bail was set at half a million. Thankfully, Mom and Jim put up their new house as collateral, which I'd helped them build. After they secured my release, Jim drove me back to their house, and during the one-hour drive, I could see the tails Ron had set up in the rearview mirrors. And just as I had predicted, I was officially on Ron's menu and I had to assume Jim's car and cell were bugged. So when Jim tried to ask me a question, I motioned for him not to say a word.

"Let the games begin," I whispered to myself, as the war kicked into gear.

It was now time to outthink Ron while he lurked in the shadows.

I assumed Ron wasn't quite ready for me, because it was too soon for him to know I'd been playing this game for almost fifteen years. This was my expertise. I was a fucking maven in the underworld. Ron was going to have to put in some long hours if he wanted a chance, because I was more determined than ever to outwork, outplay, and outlast him.

WHEN WE ARRIVED HOME, Mom made me some three-bean soup and surprisingly didn't say much, except that she was embarrassed to see my arrest on both the local news channels and ESPN, alongside Missy. I didn't say it, but I was proud to make national news. Plus, our conversation was short, because Jim must have warned her the house could have been bugged after I'd just hushed him in the driveway when he said: "Get that cash out of my basement. I can't be associated with whatever you're involved in." I then proceeded to tell Jim a parabolic microphone may be pointed our way and to keep quiet. I'm not sure if he knew what that meant, but he could sense war was on the horizon and I was on the lookout.

THAT NIGHT, I slipped out the back door of Mom's and into the dark. I carried a bike from the garage, through the woods, to a nearby road, and as soon as I hit the pavement, I fiercely pedaled to an associate's house. I was relieved to see him ready to assist in any way possible, and I immediately instructed him to get some gasoline and burn several wooden crates I'd used in a prior California run. The crates were identical to the ones Ron had already confiscated, and were located at one of my other stash houses in Saratoga, which I didn't dare go near, because I needed to become invisible, more than I'd been in the past.

I made it back to Mom's by midnight, with two new burners my associate had given me, which would help me get back on my feet, because there was no way I was quitting. Not until I was dead or in jail. I still had something to prove. The problem was, I didn't know to whom. I only knew it was my biggest struggle, probably the biggest one I had all my life. It was a feeling like I had to prove myself to others in order to be accepted, and that's what kept me grinding—approval from the outside world. I think that's what keeps us all grinding, aside from survival and passion.

THE NEXT DAY, I obtained a rental car and went back to living in my main Saratoga house. The Feds had thoroughly searched it top to bottom. They had even disconnected my TV from the wall mount and confiscated it. I was surprised to find they had left around $100,000 in the back of one of the kitchen drawers, and for a moment, I thought it was a trap, but that thought quickly dissipated. I figured they'd simply missed it, so I took $4,000 from the stack, drove to Best Buy, and purchased a new TV. This is why I always kept a locked but empty safe in my house. It was a good decoy for my best hiding places, the ones that were in plain sight.

I spent the next couple of days calling, meeting, and interviewing several local criminal defense attorneys. I had difficulty getting the word "criminal" to resonate with me, and I couldn't believe all the lawyers in Upstate New York were such pushovers. The most common thing I heard was, "Wow, it looks like you're in some big trouble." I couldn't believe none of them understood the merits of my case, but after I repeatedly found myself to be the smartest person in the room, I decided to expand my search nationwide for either a super lawyer who knew the law or a slick lawyer who knew the judge.

Unfortunately, I lacked the connections to find a lawyer who golfed with the judge, but I did find a heavy-hitting legal firm located on Park Avenue in NYC. Their address alone seemed intimidating, and I quickly deduced they were the first step toward safety, because Park Avenue was known to be one of the most affluent real estate streets in the world. It was lined with money, and where there's money, there's power.

"Eric, the first thing you must know is, we don't represent government cooperators," Michael Kennedy, Esq. said. He sat across from me at his handcrafted mahogany conference table, in his handmade Italian suit. "If you're in agreement with that, then we'd be happy to represent you."

I wasn't sure if that was Kennedy's sales pitch or his morals speaking. Regardless, he was the type of soldier I was seeking. A nationally renowned criminal defense attorney.

"It's a relief to hear that. I haven't spoken to the government and I understand the code of silence," I replied, affirming my pledge of allegiance to my organization.

"Good, now you should know, you haven't even been indicted. All they have is a complaint against you. Their case seems weak," Kennedy said slowly, with his elbows on the table, combing his fingers through his slicked-back, light gray hair. I watched as he continued to skim the search warrant to my house. "It seems their evidence is fruit of a poisonous tree," he added.

Kennedy was tall and slender, around seventy, and looked like a mob boss in his three-piece, pinstriped suit. He had an impressive track record, too. He had represented Donald Trump's former wife, Ivana, during their divorce; Native American protesters at Wounded Knee; Timothy Leary, the LSD guru; Mr. Gotti Senior, the mob boss; along with many other prominent figures. Plus, he owned *High Times* magazine, whose headquarters was across the corridor from where we were sitting. I verified this when I exited the elevator on the sixteenth floor and faintly smelled smoked weed emitting from the door labeled "Trans-High Corporation."

"So how'd the government obtain a search warrant? I didn't offload any weed from Missy's trailer," I asked, eager to understand my position and test Kennedy's reaction time.

I was slightly concerned that Kennedy's older age could be a problem. Indeed, he did have a powerful and intimidating presence, but his reaction time seemed a little sluggish to sway a courtroom full of jurors. He looked ready for retirement.

"According to this search warrant, it seems the DA misled the judge," piped in David Holland, who was sitting to Kennedy's left. "He repeatedly mentions the traffic stop of the marijuana-filled trailer and then briefly states you unloaded 'items' from the trailer, failing to clarify the only item you actually unloaded from the trailer was a dirt bike—not marijuana. It's unethical conduct, and the DA could be disbarred for that."

I lit up like a pinball wizard. I liked Dave's speed. He served as "of counsel" to Kennedy and was almost thirty years his junior. I could tell he was as sharp as a tack, and I already knew he had extensive and successful experience fighting RICO cases. Dave knew the laws of the dynamic marijuana industry better than anyone. He was counsel to *High Times,* and both the executive director and legal director of Empire State NORMAL (National Organization for the Reform of Marijuana Laws). He was hungry to win, and quickly dismissed all my apprehension over Kennedy's fatigued neurotransmitters. I instantly felt that the two of them together would be unstoppable. Plus, they had an elite private investigator whom I was told would be joining our team in the near future, to put pressure on Ron and his team.

As I continued to peruse the search warrant with Dave and Kennedy, I learned what had happened during the ill-fated cross-country trip. Missy had subbed the California drive out to her massage therapist, for a measly $3,000. I had paid Missy $60,000 to do the run each time, but now realized she'd misled me. She flew into Albany International Airport, took the trailer from her massage therapist, and then drove half an hour north to meet me in Saratoga, in hopes I wouldn't realize she hadn't completed the entire drive herself. The massage therapist, whom I'd never met, had been pulled over in Illinois for speeding, and the trailer was searched because she'd misplaced the vehicle registration. She then cooperated with law enforcement to complete a controlled delivery of the weed-loaded trailer to Missy. As Dave explained all this to me, I cringed at my stupidity for allowing Missy back into my operation. But I had no excuse for my position; I was officially a product of my choices. Every thought I'd ever had, every word I'd ever spoken, and every decision I'd ever made had brought me right there—sitting in front of two criminal defense attorneys. I guess Mom was right when she said, "You better burn your bad habits before they burn you."

Kennedy requested a half-million dollars for his team to start pretrial services, which was more than I'd anticipated, because when Ron had searched my Saratoga house, he'd stumbled across a lease to another home of mine in California, which he'd promptly searched. There he had recovered an additional $700,000 of mine, and Kennedy said this expanded the scope of the investigation, increasing his workload. On top of that, I was in a predicament because Kennedy wouldn't take a briefcase full of cash. That was hard to accept, because the Feds had frozen my bank accounts, brokerage accounts, and real estate holdings. So cash was my only option, and I needed to quickly figure out how to launder it under the watchful eye of Ron. The only thing I knew was that it was going to cost me a premium to clean it, but that's what my war chest was for—to save me from the enemy.

LATER THAT EVENING, I parked my rental car on a quiet side street in Greenpoint, Brooklyn. I needed to make contact with Streets, without notifying the Feds of our connection and his existence. My plan was simple: park a mile away from his loft apartment located on the East River, lock my burners in the trunk of the car so I couldn't be pinged, walk an indirect route to his place, stop periodically behind corners of buildings to see if I was being followed, and keep an eye open for any suspicious vehicles. My other countermeasure was to discreetly leave a tiny, unnoticeable piece of clear scotch tape on the crack of my car trunk, where it opened. If it was disturbed when I returned, I'd know the Feds had accessed my car, either to bug it or check my new burners.

There wasn't any traffic or activity surrounding the desolate warehouse that Streets lived in. The only movement was the dim flickering streetlights, with clouds of insects swarming around them. I knew if Streets was home, I would only be interrupting him doing one of two things . . . an escort or bong hits. So I spent a couple minutes throwing pebbles at his third-story window, in hopes to draw his attention.

"Jesus, hold on," Streets mumbled, after he opened his

window and looked down at me standing on the sidewalk. He looked agitated.

When Streets stepped onto the sidewalk, he stared at me bug-eyed, not saying a word. He was nervous. I could sense fear trickling through his mind. He must have seen news of my arrest, and assumed I was wired to set him up.

"Relax, I wasn't followed and I'm not wired. Search me if you want," I said, hoping he'd either pat me down or trust me so we could get down to business. "I only have a couple minutes, so snap out of it," I added.

"You shouldn't be here; make it quick," he said, looking around to make sure no one was nearby.

"My legal fees will be through the roof by the time my case is over. I need my paperwork. I can have my associate come get it tomorrow," I replied, requesting the $160,000 he owed me, without using any incriminating words to spook him more.

Streets glared at me, searching for a response.

"Relax, shit will get easier once you accept it," he eventually said.

I glared back at him. This wasn't a time for Dr. Phil. I started wondering if he was developing an excuse not to pay me.

Streets began pacing around, then reached into his pocket, pulled out a tiny piece of paper, and handed it to me, saying, "Here, call this number from a secure line tomorrow. He'll have your paperwork."

I took a breath of relief. The piece of paper had a phone number on it.

"Thank you, brother. I may not see you for a long time. Please keep the dream alive," I said, reaching out to him for a quick brotherly hug.

"I got you, stay strong. Things will be set up for you when you get out of this."

As I walked back to my car, I reflected upon Streets's words. They were leaving me with hope for a plan we had often discussed. We were going to build a retreat center near the equator, for people lost in money and drugs. We always said the business would be a success, because at the very least, we'd be full-time customers, and satisfied customers—the best business strategy of all.

When I returned to my car, the scotch tape hadn't been altered, so I assumed Ron wasn't going to waste any more manpower following me on foot until he had all his ducks in a row. But once he did, I knew he'd start firing.

DURING MY DRIVE home from NYC, I detoured to meet two other customers and instructed them on how to pay their outstanding balances. I wasn't sure if or when I'd see them again, and I don't think they did either because they'd seen the news stating I was facing five to forty years—which was a kick in the face for all of us because they needed me free, because they needed weed. The problem was, I couldn't risk making any moves, and since I couldn't, they both asked for an introduction to my suppliers, but I had to decline, because I didn't know who I could trust.

That was the first night I could remember driving home from NYC without duffel bags of cash and my stereo blasting. It was a depressing drive as I thought about all the time I had wasted living in the future, hoping my life would be better when I had this or that. I didn't question why I'd spent so many years living in the future, but in hindsight, I know why I did. It was because I felt inadequate as a child, and in order to compensate for that inadequacy, I assumed that I had to have piles of money in order to be considered successful. But that was no longer a sustainable way to live. It was merry-go-round and I was done with it. There was no point in having a job I wasn't passionate about, just to keep up with the Joneses. The Joneses were dying anyway. They had no "time." They were in the same delusional vortex as I was. Sure, having money was the way of the rich, but having free time was the way of the wealthy. Fuck, it was time to make some changes. I needed to find a career I enjoyed and to stop worrying about what I needed to "fit in." Plus, I didn't care about fitting in anymore. What I really needed was a break, and I'm not talking about a vacation. I'm talking about taking a break from people. People who told me how to live, based on how they were told to live.

22

HIGH-PROFILE

I 've worked with people from all corners of the globe, but I've never met anyone as intimidating as my private investigator, Tim Wilson. He was the son of Clyde Wilson, one of the most famous private investigators of all time, who once received a presidential pardon from Gerald Ford. He was also a former law enforcement officer in Houston and was introduced to me by Dave and Kennedy. His job was to investigate the government on my behalf, find the smoking gun, and neutralize any testimony that could be used against me in a trial. Everything about him said badass: his slicked-back, salt and pepper hair, his Robert Graham sport shirt with one-of-a-kind embroideries, his well-polished alligator boots, and his watch, which had enough gears to induce a hypnotic trance.

"Nice to meet you. Dave and Kennedy speak highly of you," I said, greeting Tim, while reaching to shake his hand.

We were on the Albany, New York FBO tarmac, and he'd just stepped out of his private jet. He called it his "rocket." He said it was the fastest-climbing jet to 41,000 feet, and it was just one of many in his fleet of planes, boats, and cars.

"You don't look like a drug dealer. They must have the wrong guy," Tim chuckled in his thick Texan accent, with a firm grip on my hand.

"Yeah, I like to blend in. It makes you less of a target," I said, watching his ears perk up as I reassured him I understood the game.

"You're in good hands, kid. We're going to put this fucking fire out," Tim replied, looking me dead in the eye.

Right then, I felt my new team forming, and I immediately felt stronger.

Tim came to take a tour of my house, hoping to find flaws in any of the direct or circumstantial evidence obtained by the DEA. I showed him where Missy's trailer had been parked in my driveway, where I offloaded the dirt bike, and where the Chevy Malibu had been parked. I knew it was a small case for him, but he took it all in, not missing any detail, because word was that he was meticulous with all his cases, which included international hostage release negotiations, jury consultations, electronic countermeasures, and covert operations. In fact, James Patterson, the thriller writer, had asked to write a book about him, but Tim was such an OG that his answer was "no."

As TIM BOARDED his jet to go meet his security detail for a high-profile billionaire client, he shouted over the wind on the tarmac, "Worst case scenario, you'll cut a deal, pay a fine, and do two years."

I instantly felt a knot in the pit of my stomach. Fuck, I wasn't ready to do two years. I'd already wasted years of my life, mostly by doing shit to fit it in ... not just on the playground, but also in my adult life. Sure, two years in a box would've been a blessing if Ron had caught me fair and square, but with the lack of evidence in hand, it felt unjust to give away any of my time.

The thought of doing prison time was unsettling, but it

inspired me to create a bulletproof narrative for the jury. Specifically one that explained exactly why I'd unloaded a dirt bike
from Missy's trailer, and coincidentally, I had one. I owned a
forty-acre parcel of land in Saratoga that was the perfect location to build a motocross track. The property already had a
clearing with about three thousand yards of dirt stockpiled in
the center of it, just enough for an excavator to build a small
track, with bermed corners, rollers, and a tabletop. So within the
week, I had the track built, and an associate of mine brought a
half-dozen semi-pro riders to practice on it, while my film crew
captured them whipping their bikes eighty-plus feet through the
air. I envisioned that presenting the jury with a professional
motocross clip would corroborate why Missy delivered a dirt
bike to my residence. I wasn't excited to lie, but with the government's bogus search warrant, deception seemed to be my only
path to safety. I pictured something along the lines of, "My name
is Eric Canori. I'm in the film industry, and I intended to film
Missy hitting some jumps at my property. When I offloaded the
dirt bike from her trailer, I didn't notice any marijuana."

WITHIN A FEW WEEKS, things started looking bright for my
defense and I could feel the pieces coming together for my
acquittal. In addition, the majority of my customers paid their
outstanding balances in full, except a couple flakes and Streets.
A call to the number Streets gave me ended with his associate
stating that Streets had nothing for me. The number soon
became invalid, and Streets had abandoned his apartment. I was
furious with his disappearance, because he had always preached
and boasted how he'd been through it all, and how reliable he
was. And now he was leaving a man down, and I couldn't believe
it. I wanted revenge, but I had to let him finish making his
mistake because I had more important shit to deal with at the

moment. Staying off Ron's radar and delivering Kennedy's check was of the essence.

I had a couple options to launder my stashed cash and get Kennedy his check. The most appealing was through my film editor, Stix, who mentioned he had an uncle who could clean cash for ten percent. The uncle owned a small construction company, and the rate was fair, considering the circumstances. Plus, Stix was trustworthy, even though he seesawed between being a chain-smoking gambler and a devout Mormon.

There was one thing that frustrated me about Stix, though. It was when I'd stop by the studio during daylight hours to work with him, and then end up finding him passed out on the couch, withering away, due to his Adderall-fueled nights. He had a good heart, though, and was more dedicated to my film project than I was. He told me his personal validation hinged upon the success of it. Actually, mine did, too. Fuck, my entire life had been centered around trying to prove my worth to others. I just never stopped to think if I was trying to be accepted for who I was or the version I was presenting—they were two different people. One presented himself as a go-getter, and the other would collapse alone at home.

"HE SAID he doesn't care where the cash came from. He'll keep his mouth shut," Stix said, late one afternoon, while taking a drag from his cigarette.

We were standing in a vacant dirt parking lot, at a trailhead, in the boondocks of Saratoga. Stix had on the same outfit as the night before, and it looked like he'd just woken.

"It's crucial for him to understand the story: he's giving me a loan to pay my legal fees. There was never any cash exchanged between us. The loan will be paid back when my assets are released from the government," I replied firmly, hoping his nicotine levels were in a comfortable range so he could comprehend the mechanics of money laundering.

"I got it and he gets it," Stix replied, adjusting his glasses over his brown sunken eyes, outlined by a pale complexion and ratty facial hair.

I was somewhat convinced he understood me, but too short on time to school him any more. It was time to do a quarter-million-dollar trial run with him and his uncle, so I quickly reached in my pocket for a burner and sent a text reading "now."

The text was sent to an associate of mine who was temporarily warehousing cash for me, two miles down the road, and who an hour earlier I had instructed to "remain on standby" and await my text confirmation before dropping $300,000 to me, which I was now going to hand over to Stix. Stix would then deliver the cash to his uncle, who lived in the neighboring town.

Stix didn't request a fee for the favor, although I included $25,000 for him as a token of my appreciation, incentive not to steal, and a friendly reminder to keep his lips sealed.

Within minutes, my associate came to a rolling stop in the dirt parking lot, popped his trunk, and remained in the car with his face covered by the brim of a baseball cap. I quickly grabbed the burgundy leather briefcase sitting inside the trunk, which I slammed shut as he accelerated off. The entire transaction took only a few seconds, and Stix instinctively didn't ask any questions.

"Make sure the check is made out to 'Michael Kennedy, P.C.' for two-fifty. I'll meet you here tomorrow at noon to retrieve it," I said, unclenching my fist from the leather handle, releasing the cash into Stix's possession. "There's an extra fifty in there for you and your uncle to split."

"Consider it done," Stix replied, swigging back his Red Bull.

His three-word reply left me feeling nervous. I was hoping he'd repeat the instructions back to me, so I knew he understood. But I didn't push it, because I didn't want him driving off to Vegas instead of his uncle's.

I needed Stix to feel important, because I knew that's what he wanted. I understood why, too. All I had to do was think about all the stupid things I did just to feel valued. And I knew if Stix didn't feel valued, he'd easily become reckless and put all my cash on "red."

I WAS DELIGHTED to see Stix with my check the following day, and I entrusted him with a couple more cash drops before he requested a short vacation in Hawaii for a self-directed detox from porn, sugar, nicotine, and consumerism.

Once Stix left town, the summer of 2009 became the most relaxing summer I'd ever had. My only obligation was to follow my pretrial release requirements, which included abstaining from illicit drugs, peeing in a cup, and remaining within New York State lines. The program was a little invasive, but it was easy to manage because I was officially retired at thirty years old and had become part of a mixed crowd of other retirees and housewives checking their mailboxes at 10 a.m. in their sweatpants, hitting the local gym at noon, and getting afternoon massages before dinner and a movie.

I also spent time fleshing out an idea I had for a software application that would allow users to surround themselves with like-minded individuals. I always had to stay busy doing something, and when I wasn't designing the user interface of my concept, I focused on personal growth and freedom. I must say, I enjoyed the leisurely lifestyle and hoped it would last forever, even though Tim Wilson said Ron was probably buying time to show my mug shot to every cooperator possible. I wasn't scared, though, because I didn't think Ron would be able to connect all the dots in my organization. Mostly because I'd abandoned that network the first day I locked eyes with him. But Ron eventually found something . . . Missy. Come late summer, the world champion, "I'm not afraid," crumbled like a dry cookie. She had told Ron everything in order for him to secure his one-count indictment, accusing us of conspiracy to possess with intent to distribute marijuana.

I was fuming. I couldn't believe Missy had decided to turn state's evidence. She had maintained a daredevil image for years, and now decided to take her mask off at my expense. She gave others up too, including Rob, who was arrested that autumn at gunpoint by over a dozen FBI and DEA agents at his home in Salt Lake City. Ron was the lead investigator on the scene, with one objective—to flip Eric.

"CAN YOU COVER MY LEGAL FEES?" Rob asked, clenching his neat Jim Beam at a dimly lit jazz bar in Manhattan.

We had just left my attorney's office, where we'd met Tim, Dave, and Kennedy for an overview of our new strategy.

"Don't worry, I'll pay them. But no matter what happens, you won't—"

Rob then cut me off with, "Come on, man. I'll never turn on you. I don't talk shit about my friends . . . not even on the worst days. I'll say one thing, though—I knew we shouldn't have trusted that rat."

Rob instantly cleared any doubts of his integrity, and then took down his entire drink in one gulp, immediately requesting another.

"Don't forget, we're innocent until proven guilty. It's her word against ours," I said, trying to calm his nerves. "Our attorneys will crucify her on the stand."

Rob seemed unconvinced, knowing his arrest could've been avoided by furnishing Ron with information about my organization. But he'd understood the job requirements before he'd ever accepted a dollar from me, and he righteously chose to face this complication with me, for one reason: because he was sticking to our agreement.

There was one way I could've saved Rob and myself. Missy's testimony could have been removed from the equation. Disappearance, missing person, fatal accident, whatever you want to call it. I was presented with two options, from two different connects. Option one, the blue-collar offer: "Anything you need, E, just say the word. We will take care of it." I didn't respond, knowing that "conspiracy" is a prosecutor's best friend. I just paused, before moving the conversation to another topic. However, if I had replied, "Do it," Missy would've been chopped into tiny pieces, flushed down a toilet, added to the missing persons list, and knockin' on heaven's door.

Option two, the white-collar offer: "People have accidents, Eric. People trip and fall all the time." I didn't reply to that offer either, because I'm not a killer. But I will admit to thinking . . . Missy broke our agreement and held others responsible for her underhanded choices—in exchange for her freedom. Basically, she surrendered my freedom, after making well over a million dollars working with me under our code of silence. I never forced her to work with me; she begged to transport my product. Every time I saw her she was asking for extra runs. The bottom line was, we had a business agreement, and usually when parties breach contracts in the multitrillion-dollar underground economy, lawyers aren't called—hit men are.

Luckily for Missy, Mom taught me to work for freedom, rather than to kill for it.

23

STAKEOUT

Hallelujah! I found a dream going into 2010. Her name was Vera, and she had been born and raised in Ukraine, but Americanized over the past fifteen years by her older and wealthy ex-husband, in a town neighboring Saratoga. Vera was a tall, healthy, olive-skinned woman —who glowed without makeup. The kind of woman who indulges in essential oils, infrared saunas, yoga, colonics, blonde highlights, and Lululemon apparel accented by full-grain leather accessories.

Her motto was: Good health is classy. For her it came down to good nutrition, exercise, rest, and a positive attitude. It was about being centered and staying centered. Her catchphrase was, "Save your money—it all starts on the inside," but I still liked to spend—mostly on our entertainment and adventures. She liked adventure, too. Every morning when we woke up, we'd do whatever popped into our mind. Our activities revolved around the weather. One day we'd be at a movie, and the next we'd be chartering a helicopter to a remote island in the Adirondacks. It was the first time I'd felt like a millionaire, because I had two things: free time and a real woman.

. . .

I WAS FLYING low over the Long Island Sound with Vera, in a private turboprop I'd chartered for a quick summer vacation in Montauk, New York. The sun's rays were illuminating the entire cabin, and the ocean was sparkling below us. Vera was sitting in one of the tan leather seats across from me, in a low-cut pink sundress.

"Are you scared?" Vera asked.

"I'm not scared," I replied, behind my Maui Jims. But who was I fooling? I'd been living in fear since I learned how to ride a tricycle. And even though the newspaper had recently reported that my case had been postponed indefinitely, Tim said the government was probably buying time to build a RICO case against me. So of course I was worried, because the RICO law allows prosecutors to extend criminal penalties for organized crime.

"Do you think you'll go to prison?" Vera asked calmly, sincerely concerned.

I didn't want to answer, because I'd hoped our vacation would delay discussing the truths surrounding our relationship. But no matter how many rare oysters we ate at white linen tablecloth restaurants, the facts always remained below the surface.

"I'll win. If not, I will on appeal," I answered, knowing Vera would focus on what could go right, rather than what might go wrong.

Vera understood thought patterns and how everything is connected. Her awareness put her at an advantage with everything in life. I think after traveling the world with her ex, she recognized that money, exotic cars, turquoise-colored waters, and rivieras can't buy lasting happiness. That's probably why we clicked. Our values complemented each other's. We'd both fulfilled many of our lavish desires before meeting, and finally realized that a peaceful evening at home with the one you love is one of the most comforting things in life.

Sharing home-cooked dinners with Vera and her younger daughter was my first experience in a peaceful family. We prepped food together, gardened, watched documentaries, and made snow angels. I drove her daughter to Waldorf School, with the promise of Vera's lips when I returned home . . . and within a year, Vera had turned me from a boy into a man. The relationship was foreign to me, because I was used to attracting women with my money. But to my surprise, I had finally attracted the woman I needed, and I felt blessed because I was sharing my life with the right woman, rather than wasting time scrolling through the wrong ones. Life was good, almost too good. I assumed something had to go wrong, sooner or later.

MY TRIAL HAD ALREADY BEEN DELAYED one and a half years, and as the delay continued into the beginning of 2011, I received a tip that Ron was conducting intensive and expensive around-the-clock surveillance on me. I was told he had been budgeted sixty days for the investigation, and that it was his last opportunity to gather substantial incriminating evidence against me, before my case was dismissed.

After the tip, I immediately grabbed a burner I had stashed in Vera's garage, drove to the local gym, got out of my car, stood in the parking lot, and popped a battery into the burner. The phone was dedicated exclusively for corresponding with Tim, and I made sure to never use it near any real estate attached to my name.

When Tim answered, our conversation was short, and he said he'd get back to me the following day at 5 p.m. to confirm if I was in the frying pan or in the fire.

. . .

"Yo," I answered. It was Tim, the following day at 5 p.m. sharp. I'd been walking around Vera's neighborhood, waiting on his call like an ambulance.

"You're in the fire. Watch your step," Tim said, in a monotone voice, verifying Ron's 24/7 surveillance on me.

I paused and looked around the residential neighborhood. There were more than two hundred newly constructed town-homes, but I didn't see anything suspicious—although there were over a hundred parked cars in sight, so anything was possible.

"Fuck, any advice?" I asked.

"Yeah, don't talk to anyone. Assume everything is being intercepted."

"Ten-four," I replied, hanging up.

I popped the battery out of the burner and looked around. Sure enough, an unfamiliar Toyota Camry with Vermont plates drove slowly by me. I knew the cars in Vera's neighborhood, and this one didn't belong. It was confirmed: I no longer had a private life. Ron was the predator and I was the assignment. And as a suspect in a federal government stakeout, the government would know what I ate, what type of laundry detergent I used, and what time I went to bed. It was a threat I couldn't avoid, but one I could strategically manage.

AFTER A WEEK OF OBSERVATION, I noticed Ron had a couple agents rotating on me at all times, which allowed them to change position more often and reduce their possibility of detection. They blended into my surrounding environment perfectly, driving boring vehicles and never making eye contact with me. It was stressful, but I laid low, played dumb, and continued life as usual. I didn't alert Vera to the investigation, or anyone else. It was important that I allowed the DEA to conduct their mission unnoticed, so they wouldn't extend it.

ARE YOU FUCKING KIDDING ME! It was 10 p.m. on a Sunday, and Max, an associate of mine who'd been warehousing cash for my legal fees, was calling on my personal iPhone. I didn't answer, even though I knew the damage was done. He'd just electronically bridged our association after I had successfully cleared Ron's sixty-day stakeout, unscathed, the week prior. I assumed it was an emergency, because Max knew to never call my personal line.

I immediately raced through the snow-covered roads to call Max back on one of the last payphones in existence. When I arrived at the gas station, I dropped eight quarters into the machine, dialed his number, and asked, "What's up?"

"Sorry I called. It was a mistake," Max replied, sounding like a drunken sailor.

I was furious. I'd paid him for one simple job: never call me, give me a key to your apartment, and allow me to leave a bag of cash in your spare bedroom closet. I've never heard of an easier job to fuck up.

"Where are you right now?" I asked.

"At my parents' house," he slurred.

"Stay there. I'll be there in ten minutes."

I knew where Max's parents lived, because I'd dropped him off in his middle-class neighborhood years ago, when he'd helped me part-time building water features.

Max was thirty-five, quiet, trustful, antisocial, and a fully functional alcoholic. Since graduating college over a decade earlier, he had maintained the same nine-to-five warehouse job and watched hockey games alone in the evenings, while packing dips and drinking vodka by the bottle. His schedule didn't deviate from that. I often wondered if he was lonely, but I never asked. I should have, though, because I knew the hardest part of being lonely is admitting it to others. It's that feeling of being afraid of what people might think. It's the fear of being judged as a loser. I think that's why I used to say, "I'm bored." It was a safer play than saying, "I'm lonely."

WHEN MAX OPENED the front door he looked pale, frail, and malnourished. I hadn't seen him in a few months due to the stakeout, but he had definitely taken a turn for the worse. He looked barely alive.

"What's wrong?" I asked, as he gripped the doorknob to prevent himself from falling over. I wanted to help, but couldn't stay long because my car was parked about twenty houses down, under the assumption Ron had a GPS tracker on it. "Please don't call me on my iPhone again. Things are hot right now."

"I'm sorry," he mumbled, barely able to speak.

His eyes were bloodshot and he reeked of booze.

"I'll get all my cash out of your apartment in a week. I'm sorry to rush, but I have to go," I said, again wishing I could help him.

I'm not sure what led Max to binge drink, but I did know his drunk dial had just put him on Ron's suspect list, and that I needed to remove all my cash from his apartment ASAP. Furthermore, I needed to launder it, because Kennedy was now certain we were headed to trial, and he needed another half-million to fight. Kennedy said even if we were lucky enough to hear "case dismissed," it wouldn't happen until the first day of trial. So I arranged to have the remaining cash at Max's apartment safely transferred to Stix's uncle the following Monday.

Stix's uncle would then resume providing checks payable to Michael Kennedy, P.C., because like Etu told me, "It's not illegal unless you get caught."

Breaking the law was taking its toll on me in more ways than I could count, but when you mix poverty, peer pressure, and drugs, you get people like me: outlaws. I tried not to view myself as an outlaw, but facts are facts. When someone's hungry and their basic needs aren't being met, it's a safe bet they'll do anything to survive.

It was Sunday, six days since Max had called and one day before I had an associate lined up to transfer my cash from Max's. I'd just stepped out of the shower to the ring of my iPhone. It was Max's brother, whom I hadn't seen or spoken to since college. I sensed trouble, but reluctantly I answered.

"Hello?" I hesitated, not forgetting my iPhone was forever tapped.

"Eric, it's Ken Nelson," he replied. Ken was also a drunkard, and I'd already anticipated his next words. "I d-d-don't know if you heard, but my b-b-brother died," he stuttered.

"No, I hadn't heard. I'm so sorry for your loss. Is there anything I can do?"

"I'm okay, but you should go see my father. He's home now."

I didn't ask, but I assumed the cause of death was alcohol poisoning.

My mind immediately started spinning on the whereabouts of my cash. I figured his father had found it when cleaning out Max's apartment, and upon noticing Max's last living call was to me, guessed it was mine. Ken had probably mentioned the rumors he'd heard of my weed sales in college.

I was exhausted upon taking Ken's call, because Vera and I had an argument the night before and I hadn't slept. But the call was the shot of adrenaline that led me to speed like Cruella de Vil to Max's apartment, to verify whether my cash was still there. And nope, it was gone. Just a bunch of half-broken rubber bands were left behind. Motherfuckers . . . wherever my cash was, they'd better not have spent one dollar, I thought. I was already furious with Vera for nagging me about the trial delays, and now Max's family had my trial funds. I was officially on the brink of snapping. To top it off, upon exiting Max's apartment I saw a manned Cadillac Escalade just down the street. But my fear was short-lived, because nothing was going to get in the way of me and my money that day. If needed, I was ready to break more laws.

I ran half a mile down the road to my car, hopped in, and sped to Max's father's house with one eye in my rearview. The coast looked clear, so I surmised the Cadillac must've been a lost civilian. I hoped I was right, because in my business you had to be right one hundred percent of the time. Because if you were right only 99.99 percent of the time, you'd go to jail.

FUCK! When Mr. Nelson opened his front door, his cheeks were rosier than Rudolph's nose. I'd never met him before, but it looked like he was a drinker too. He was shaking. I assumed it was booze.

"Hi, Mr. Nelson."

He didn't respond. He looked as if he was going to fall over, but I wasn't about to call 9-1-1.

"I'm so sorry for your loss," I added, standing in the crusty snow on his front porch. "Ken informed me of the situation. I understand this is a tough time, but I left something very important in Max's apartment, and I need it back, please," I said calmly, trying to show solidarity for his loss.

"That's out of my hands now," he replied.

"Excuse me!" I snapped back, starting to boil inside. "Can you please be more specific?"

"I can't get it back. I'm sorry, it's gone."

I hold my anger well, but my deadline for Kennedy's check was less than forty-eight hours away, and I was starting to sense a major problem, because I already had the cash transfer scheduled for the following day.

I started walking in small circles on the porch, thinking and biting my tongue, in case he had a wire on. I was fuming. I wasn't sure what to do. Part of me wanted to hold a combat knife to his throat, but lucky for him, Jim had taught me to be subservient in times of "tough luck." So I calmly replied, "With all due respect, Mr. Nelson, I'm sorry for your loss, but please understand, I'm involved in a very serious, costly legal battle, and I need my things back now."

After a few minutes of pleading with Mr. Nelson, he finally came around to, "I'm sorry. I didn't know. The money is in my friend's safe. I can get it for you tomorrow."

I took a breath of relief, and told Mr. Nelson I'd be back the following day at 7 p.m. to retrieve it.

My plan was to have an associate come with me, so I could pass the cash off to him, and he could then transport the cash to Stix's uncle, since Stix was away in LA nurturing some of our film connections, who'd just gotten off tour with Snoop Dogg.

I had wished Stix was in Saratoga. I could've used his help because I was done with the bullshit, and the days of me being kind were over. Actually, it's fair to say I was close to my breaking point, which was something I'd never hit, because no matter how much pressure I'd ever encountered, I always came back to center. There were no exceptions, because I was trained to stay calm in any and all unpredictable situations. It was a skill I had to learn through countless crises, and a skill I learned by starting from scratch. It's called resilience, and I was a master at it. But if these drunkards decided to stiff me, I was now at a point where I wasn't going to walk away politely.

24

SACRIFICES

I was cooking breakfast at home and had barely slept in the last forty-eight hours. My face was sunken and I looked like a madman. I was exhausted, but I wasn't going to be able to sleep in peace until Kennedy was paid in full, which was scheduled to happen later that night. I had already confirmed the logistics with my associate, who'd assist me in picking up the cash from Mr. Nelson at 7 p.m., then deliver it to Stix's uncle on my behalf.

I'd had only one bite of my eggs when my iPhone rang. I couldn't believe it. It was Mr. Nelson, after I'd specifically told him not to call me.

"Hello," I answered, hesitantly.

"Eric, I have it. Now's the only time you can come over. My wife will be home later," Mr. Nelson faltered, as I trembled to his words. "I'll leave it in my garage for you. The side door is open."

I was speechless. I was certain the blockhead had just left a nice tip over my tapped iPhone for Ron's investigation.

"Thank you," I eventually said. "I'll be there in ten minutes."

My only option was to pick up the cash on my own. I had no time to wait for my associate. The cash needed to be retrieved, immediately, before Ron potentially staked out Mr. Nelson's house. It was Lone Ranger time.

As I sped to Mr. Nelson's, I gripped the steering wheel tightly, but the tighter I gripped, the less control I had.

While stopped at a red light, I said a quick prayer to protect me from Ron during the thirty-minute drive I'd be making to Stix's uncle. It went something like, "Dear Universe which art in Space, forgive me for my trespasses that have led me into temptation. I promise never to hurt anyone, for ever and ever. Please protect my cash."

I wasn't the type of guy to pray often, but I knew some religious words from when Mom had me attend Catholic school from age five to ten.

WHEN I ARRIVED at Mr. Nelson's garage, I didn't see a duffel bag containing my $450,000 anywhere. I double-checked both bays and in between all his landscaping equipment. Out of places to look, I lightly knocked on the door, leading into the house. After waiting a minute and not hearing any movement from inside, I stepped away to exit the garage and try the front doorbell. Just before stepping out of the garage, I heard the door open behind me. And there was Mr. Nelson, walking toward me with my bag held high like a prize.

A smile of relief instantly rushed to my face.

"Thank you so much, you saved me," I said, as he handed me the duffel bag. "Please let me know if there's anything I can do for you or your family."

He didn't reply, because he was shoved to the side.

"Down on the ground! Down on the ground! Down on the fuckin' ground, now!" Ron screamed, storming out of the house, through the pedestrian door, into the garage, shoving Mr. Nelson aside, pointing the barrel of his twelve-gauge shotgun in my face faster than a jack-in-the-box. Five other agents followed right behind, in full tactical gear, with their Glocks out, all pointed at me. Ron was so pumped, I could see his teeth vibrating and gums salivating.

"Okay! Okay! Jesus!" I yelled, with surprise and fright, almost peeing myself. I was on the ground, hands out, shaking like a puppy on the Fourth of July. My heart was pounding. I must have prayed to the wrong god. "What's going on?" I asked.

"Get up! We're going to go have a little talk," Ron said, as his partners yanked me off the ground and cuffed my wrists.

It felt like a bad dream. Nothing felt real. I tried to snap out of it, but I couldn't. My compounded exhaustion had completely distorted all my decision-making abilities. I'd missed all the obvious signals that Mr. Nelson was setting me up. What the fuck was he thinking reporting the cash to law enforcement? It wasn't a bomb. It was just cash. He could've at least assumed it was a going-away present from Max, and shared it with his wife. I was at a loss for words. Between the pressure from Kennedy, Vera, Ron, and Max, I had become so fatigued that my mind had completely unraveled. Fuck, I was spent. I was dying trying to act stronger than I actually was. I know a certain amount of stress is healthy, but I was experiencing an exorbitant amount of it. I felt jittery. My stress was no longer working properly, because when it did, it helped me avoid rookie mistakes like this. It helped me stay focused and alert, so I could survive all the predators on the road to success.

It's fair to say it was a shitty day. Beneath a dull, gloomy, sunless sky, the DEA had me, and Ron packed me in the back of a patrol car and escorted me to his headquarters in Albany.

Technically I hadn't committed a crime, because receiving a duffel bag full of cash is not illegal unless it can be proven in a court of law that it's part of an illicit activity. However, anyone can be held in police custody for up to twenty-four hours, without being charged with a crime. It's a tactic regularly used by law enforcement to scare suspects into confessions.

As I rode solo in the back seat, with my hands cuffed behind my back, I remembered I had a burner in my front jacket pocket, along with a small piece of paper with Stix's uncle's address on it. I'd forgotten I'd placed them there the day before. If Ron acquired these items, he could potentially link the duffle bag of cash to a money laundering charge and I'd be more fucked than I already was. So it was imperative that I get them off my person, and that's what I tried to do. I tried by discreetly trying to fish them out of my pocket whenever the patrol car accelerated and the engine's RPM increased. My hope was that the sound of the engine would cover the sound of me wiggling my arms around to reach both items and stuff them into the crack of the rear seat. But no, the patrol car came to a complete halt, and the agent in the front passenger seat unbuckled, reached around back, frisked me, and confiscated my phone, wallet, and the piece of paper.

I was fucked. I definitely couldn't put this day on my resume. Within one week, I had fully mastered the right way to do everything completely wrong. I had no more excuses. This is who I was, and these were my results.

SOON ENOUGH, I found myself sitting at a steel table in a ten-by-ten windowless room, with a fluorescent light above. It was the interrogation room you see in all the movies, where they play good cop/bad cop with the threat to society.

"I need to call my lawyer," I said.

"Relax, you can call your lawyer, but I want to tell you something first," Ron replied, calm and collected. "I know a lot of people owe you money. If you help me get that money, this can all go away."

I wasn't sure if Ron could see the "fuck you" in my face, because I did my best not to show it, as he was playing the "nice cop." His angle was, let's be partners and get revenge on your enemies. But I wasn't buying it, so I continued to remain silent.

That's when the "bad cop" stormed into the room, slamming his hand on the table, yelling in my face, "You think anyone is going to believe you made this cash building waterfalls? You're going to prison for a very, very long time! We know everything! This is your last and final chance to work with us!" We locked eyes, but I knew the louder he yelled, the less he truly knew. His angle was clear, too. Stop giving a fuck about people who no longer add value to your life and save *yourself* now. But I wasn't buying that, either, and he was furious as he stormed out of the room so Ron could come back in and try to finish their job.

Ron entered the room.

"Eric, there comes a time in life when it's smarter to be loyal to your future than your past, and now's that time," Ron tried again, playing the role of Mr. Miyagi.

Ron was wise. I wished I could've paid him off right then and there, but he was wasting his time because I wasn't going to cooperate in any form. I'd pledged allegiance to my organization long before I was on Ron's radar. I was nervous, though, because I could sense his entire team in the background gathering information on the address they'd found in my pocket, and I knew it was just a matter of time before they'd race to Stix's uncle's house and try to squeeze him, too. I could only pray to a different god he wouldn't flip, because Ron couldn't prove anything if everyone sealed their lips.

I didn't know much about Stix's uncle, but I've found the best way to test someone's loyalty is when they're behind your back and out of sight. And that's exactly where Stix's uncle was, while I sat alone in a holding tank, with my fingers crossed, for several hours, at the DEA headquarters.

I did my best to calm myself, but I couldn't stop the thoughts racing through my head. Would Stix's uncle jump ship to save himself? Was he the type of soldier to leave a man down? Did he know you shouldn't break trust and promises? Did he have the resilience and perseverance to operate in a world that thrives not only in good times but, most importantly, in strenuous times? Only time would tell if his actions matched his words. In the meantime—between what I felt and what I knew—I was fucked.

25

SHACKLED

I definitely hadn't found the right god to pray to, because later that night I was booked into the Rensselaer County Jail. I assumed Stix's uncle had folded, because I was placed in the highest security unit, with an abundance of surveillance cameras overhead. The unit housed twenty-four inmates, many of them facing twenty-five to life for homicide, armed robbery, or assault with a deadly weapon. There were also several repeat drug offenders there. I think this was Ron's way of giving me a sneak peek into what the next couple decades of my life could look like if I didn't work with him.

The following day, I was escorted in shackles to my court hearing, and Dave Holland met me there.

It was a good thing I never promised Vera I'd always be by her side, because the judge deemed me a flight risk and denied my bail. I was charged with money laundering and Dave informed me that Ron's squad did in fact raid Stix's uncle's house and flipped him quicker than an IHOP short stack. His uncle had told Ron everything, and Ron immediately flew to LA for Stix, who sang like a canary, too. I wasn't even surprised that their loyalty could shift so easily; I was simply exhausted. Sure, I had made a thousand good moves, but all it took was a few bad ones to drop me to my knees. Even so, I wasn't surrendering. That would've involved quitting, and quitting wasn't an option.

VERA LOOKED hotter than a pistol on our first jail visit. She always wore simple, yet revealing outfits for me. She knew I didn't like lots of designs and patterns. I preferred clean lines, because they allowed me to focus on who she was, rather than what she had.

"I'm sorry . . . ," I said to Vera, through the grated porthole of the thick glass partition.

Vera knew not to say anything incriminating. Instead, she gently pressed the palm of her hand flat against the glass, matching it to mine. It was our form of reconciliation, after a week of turmoil that I'd initiated.

I couldn't help thinking Ron's snitches were probably home with their loved ones eating bonbons, purchased with my money, while I was stuck—wanting one last kiss from Vera—before I went back to war.

"How can I help? They wouldn't allow me to bring food in for you," Vera replied.

This was why I loved Vera so much. It was her forward-thinking. She always focused on what could be done, rather than what had been done.

"Can you please mail me my *Master Key* book and a picture of you?" I requested, knowing jail was my new home.

I didn't have time to exchange many words with Vera during our quick visit. However, she did mention three guys had dropped by her house in FBI jackets, with badges and questions. But like any good partner would, she responded with, "Sorry, I'm unable to help."

Vera was a trooper, and she finally understood the magnitude of my case and could feel the tension surrounding me. Neither of us said it, but we both recognized there was a possibility we'd never touch each other again. It was a stinging thought, but a valid one. The last thing Vera said was, "I love you." That's when we both began to tear up, and the tears were real, the ones that come from the heart. Vera's tears ran over her cheekbones and onto her jaw, and mine puddled in my eyes. We loved each other.

Ron had just landed a heavy blow. It was the biggest piece he could take from me. Vera, my love, my most brilliant achievement to date.

As I pushed myself away from the glass partition, I didn't know when I'd see Vera again, and it was difficult to walk away through the tears. I wanted to go home with her. I craved her touch. Our intimacy was certified authentic. It had flowered from morning meditations into all-day sex marathons, where Vera taught me about the power of sexual energy. She explained to me how it's the most potent form of energy available to men, and she taught me how to use it to supercharge my life. She said that every time I ejaculated, I lost life force energy, but explained it was the opposite for her, because women only lose life force energy during menstruation and childbirth.

I'd still be in and out of Vera all day, almost exploding each time, but instead of using my energy to replenish my seeds, Vera would remind me to retain them for days on end, in order to notice how much more productive and driven I'd become. And when I didn't release, I could open subtle channels that'd carry the energy up my spine, to my brain, and back down. If we were in a session long enough, I could get an orbit of energy flowing that would harmonize my body into a blissful state. It was a strategy that increased my mental clarity and gave me the energy to conquer any undertaking outside of the bedroom, except for one thing—Ron, the ultimate test.

26

ONE-MAN ARMY

"**E**ric, things don't look good. We were in a strong position before, but now with the money laundering charge, we're in an uphill battle," Kennedy said, on his first inmate legal visit with Dave.

Our conversation was taking place in a small concrete room, with a large glass window facing the guards.

"Have Tim find Stix and his uncle. We need them to shut their mouths. They need to understand the burden of proof lies on the government," I pleaded.

"We've tried, but it's too dangerous. They're fully cooperating with the government and their attorney won't return our calls. Our other problem is that I'm implicated in the money laundering charge, since the checks were payable to me," Kennedy replied.

I sat speechless. There had to be some positive news. Anything to remind me why I'd already paid him over $700,000. But he had nothing else to say either.

"So, what are you telling me?" I eventually asked.

"With the new conflict of interest, I have to formally dismiss myself from your case. But Dave will remain on board, and I'll advise him from the background."

My face froze, my heart sank, and my ego folded. The news of abandonment had come at exactly the wrong time. Actually, I've found there's never a right time for bad news. That's probably why Mom always said: "Buckle up, buttercup."

"So what's the strategy going forward?" I asked Kennedy, searching for a solution.

"It's time for you to cooperate, then I can get you out of here tomorrow."

"What?!"

"Relax. Once you're out, you'll have more freedom to do things our way. You won't need to fully help them: just pretend, put on a show, make an effort, have brain fog, and then quit helping."

I couldn't believe what I was hearing, but Kennedy was as serious as a heart attack. I was speechless, but Dave whispered there could be a camera reading our lips, so before I said another word, I followed suit by covering my mouth with my hand. In addition, I started shuffling my feet to drown out our voices.

"I'm not working for them," I whispered.

Kennedy looked at me over the rim of his glasses as if I were thickheaded.

"Well that's a poor choice, Eric, but if that's it, Dave needs to get paid for the trial."

"I'll have someone get you a check soon," I replied.

I had nothing else to say, and he had nothing else to tell me. Our allotted time was up anyway.

As the guards escorted me back to my cell, I realized I'd just been whittled down to a one-man army and barricaded by Ron on all sides. Last I knew, Tim was preparing to hand-deliver sixteen subpoenas to the DEA agents involved in my initial arrest. But now Kennedy said Tim also envisioned my trial being a loss. I didn't want to believe it, but Ron had separated all my forces and brought me right back to my childhood, sitting alone in a room, with no clear way out.

Who was I fooling? I'd be hard-pressed to get Dave a check without access to my buried war chest. No one knew where it was but me. Plus, Kennedy was now basically saying the verdict would be "guilty," so I was just buying time to think, because like Jim always said, "Never reply to anyone when you're angry."

I was angry to the point where no one could save me. Not a doctor, not a cell phone, not a lawyer, and not a family member. I was trapped, for what felt like the hundredth time. There was a difference this time, though, because my money was no longer important to me. What I really craved was *time*. More time to enjoy the simple things. More time to be free. I was tired of counting money, and I was tired of keeping score. What the fuck was the point of piles of cash if I had no time to spend it?

What I really needed in life was balance. I needed to enjoy the fruits of my labor before I turned to dust. I needed to spend more time on things that would make me feel whole and complete. I think this is something rich people realize on their deathbed, but for me I was realizing it on my prison bed. And what really struck a chord in me was when I acknowledged that I'm not going to make it out of this life alive. That's when I closed my eyes and asked for a second chance. A second chance at life, because I definitely wasn't prepared for my first.

27

LOST DREAMS

I t didn't take long to settle into my jail routine: Wake up at 6:30 a.m., oatmeal for breakfast, newspaper for current events, push-ups for strength, shower for alertness, fake hamburger for lunch, write a letter to Vera, walk in circles, SPAM for dinner, then read. And thankfully, Vera mailed the original version of *The Master Key System*, by Charles Haanel. The book is considered by many to be the greatest self-development book ever written. It's over one hundred years old and teaches the importance of truth, harmonious thinking, and the ability to concentrate. Rumor has it that the book inspired Bill Gates to drop out of Harvard and put a computer on every desk in the world. That's some serious power—the type I needed to get out of jail. It's also why I studied one of the twenty-four lessons contained within the book every night before bed, while visualizing and focusing on my freedom.

When I wasn't in my cell reading or sleeping, I spent time in the common area outside my cell mingling with other inmates, because there was a hierarchy in jail, and I had to establish myself in it. My place would be determined by what crime I had committed and how respectful I was to other inmates. Luckily for me, murderers and big-time drug dealers were considered heroes, while rapists and child molesters were considered lowlifes. And while the lowlifes remained in extreme danger, heroes were respected. So once the other inmates had confirmed the nature and magnitude of my crime, I had no reason to watch my back with fear. Instead, I could look forward with hope.

"QUIT STRESSING, E," Terry said, an inmate who claimed he was innocent, but was also being held without bail for allegedly stabbing someone who had robbed him.

Terry was a black guy, about my age, but much stronger than me. He was playing chess with another inmate in the common area, and I was standing, hovering over their game, contemplating the next phone call I'd be making to Dave. I knew Dave would be asking about the status of his check.

"I'm not stressin'," I replied, remaining in my head, thinking about how I could legally furnish Dave with a half-million-dollar check.

"You better not say that to your judge," Terry said, moving his queen diagonally.

They both laughed simultaneously, and so did I—sort of.

"Do you guys know anything about Judge Sharpe?" I asked.

Sharpe was the judge assigned to my case.

"Oh shit! You have 'The Time Machine'?" Terry asked, looking up from the board toward me.

"What do you mean?"

"They call Sharpe 'The Time Machine' because anyone that stands before him gets sentenced closer to the maximum. You better have a good lawyer, my friend."

I shivered into a stiff freeze as the voices of the inmates in the background faded into a distant echo. I felt I was slowly being sucked into a vacuum with my tiny memories and lost dreams. Fuck, was I really going to spend the next few decades in a cell, just for weed and money laundering? I had never said, "When I grow up . . . I want to be a drug dealer."

As I walked back to my cell in silence, I felt empty. I was going to miss Vera more than my cash and freedom.

I needed help. I needed some form of mercy. Actually, all of the inmates needed help, because we were all going through shit just like everyone goes through shit. It just comes down to how much of it sticks to us, and whether or not we recognize, beneath all that shit, we all secretly love each other. It's called universal love, and it's the harmony of everyone and everything in the universe.

28

REALIGNMENT

"Eric, I got Jim's check, thank you. When will I get the rest?" Dave said, during our second jail visit—after Jim had sent him $10,000 on my behalf to buy me more time.

"I'm working on it. I'll have an update soon," I replied with confidence.

"Okay, good. Also, I wanted to tell you something in person so you wouldn't worry," Dave said, pausing. "Rob pled out yesterday, but he took a safety valve."

My face froze. Rob knew a lot about my organization, and I immediately wanted to know how much he had told them.

"Relax. A safety valve means he gave a statement about his involvement, but he will not testify against you."

I took a breath. "So is Rob still in our corner?" I eagerly asked.

"Yes, I spoke with his lawyer. He's still out on bail, but he won't hurt us."

Rob knew a lot about my organization, but I quickly convinced myself he wasn't a liability. He was clever and had been in enough skiing accidents to claim 'source amnesia' and only would have confirmed what Missy had told them. He knew it wasn't perjury to say, "I don't recall."

"One other thing . . . Ron called me today. He said if you help him get someone by the name of 'Cora,' you can get out of here tomorrow," Dave said.

"She's a nobody." I paused, wondering why Ron wanted Cora. "She wasn't involved with the confiscated weed. It came from another Cali source. I stopped dealing with Cora months before my arrest."

"Well, did Missy know her?"

"Yeah, she met her once. But I'll rot away in here before I give anyone up," I replied.

Fucking Missy. It seemed she'd told Ron about Cora, too. This was the exact reason why I didn't want Cora smoking bowls with Missy in the driveway.

From day one, I had strategically designed the supply chain of my organization so operators at any one link in the chain were unaware of all the other links and operators. I implemented this strategy to protect all the individuals in my organization, in the event of any one person being compromised by law enforcement.

I know my rules and approach seemed stiff to Cora, but it was now confirmed; she had started digging her grave when she'd ignored my rules and talked to Missy in that California driveway. If she had known better and had listened to me, she would've accepted I was the boss on that deal, and that I didn't have time to attend every argument I was invited to.

AFTER A COUPLE WEEKS of being locked up, I was allowed contact visits twice per week, and Jim and Vera were at the top of my list. Without the glass partition between us, we could finally converse privately.

The first thing I asked Jim was to sell the house I had helped build for him and Mom, in order to cover my trial fees. But he said Mom wouldn't go for it, which was a hard pill to swallow. And even though I had gold buried in their yard, I couldn't tell them that, because Ron was watching them, too. I knew so, because he and his crew searched their house after my last arrest. I'm not sure how that search warrant was obtained; maybe because I had three-bean soup there. Regardless, Ron was watching everyone close to me, and I didn't think things could get much worse.

Fuck! I thought too soon. It was the following week, and Stix came to visit me wearing a wire. I could tell Ron had him by the balls, too. I could see the fear in his micro-expressions.

I avoided saying anything incriminating to Stix during our recorded conversation, and I didn't call him out on his weakness. But he eventually acknowledged with a wink that I knew he was wired, and it took an immense amount of self-control to restrain myself from ripping off his shirt and yelling into the wire, "Ron I know you're out there! You fucking weasel!" Needless to say, I didn't stay in the visit long, because my expectations of Stix had quickly turned to frustration, and that frustration had quickly turned to silence. A bitter silence.

With my silence came a newfound advantage over Ron: *The Master Key System*. The book's exercises started leading me toward a superior intelligence on higher planes than I'd ever fathomed existed, and I studied the book religiously in my cell every day, for hours on end. The book aligned me with the power I'd been seeking. It connected me to the natural laws of the universe. It was the most powerful book I'd ever read. It prompted the crystallization of logical thought patterns across my mind, and it began replacing all the uncertainties in my life

—with predictability. Most importantly, it helped me see clearly into Ron's thoughts and all the moves I needed to make to get out of jail. Ron didn't want me in jail; he wanted awards, well-fed kids, a happy wife, and all my fucking money.

Ron knew a lot about me, but there was one thing he didn't know. Being locked in a room as a child had been more difficult than being locked in a cell. Of course I missed Vera, but oddly enough, I felt safer in my cell now than I did during my childhood. And I knew if I could indicate to Ron that I was comfortable in jail, I could essentially force his hand. However, I only had one line of verbal communication with him: the monitored inmate phone system.

I knew Ron listened to each of my inmate phone calls on repeat, fiending for Eric Canori clues. Therefore they would be the perfect avenue for my simple plan to break Ron down, to frustrate him, to make him lose sleep, and to flip his tactics back onto him without him ever realizing it. I'd appear strong, even though I was at my weakest point. The game would take an indefinite amount of time for proper execution, but if my partners knew how to play, Ron would never call my bluff. The end goal would be to make a deal with Ron on my terms. The deal would be about freedom. Freedom to live how I wanted to live.

VERA BECAME MORE alluring with each jail visit. Her presence held the attention of all the guards in the visiting room, but there was only one thing that held her attention—perseverance, the recipe to all my wins.

"I think I know a way out, Beautiful," I whispered over Vera's right cheek.

The visitation rules prevented us from touching, but allowed us to sit on stools with a low partition between us.

"I'm sure you do, my love," Vera said with a grin, loving how I could go from one failure to another, without loss of enthusiasm.

"Please listen carefully, because the slightest mistake can ruin the entire plan. We need to portray to the DEA that we don't have a problem being separated for a long time," I replied, lasering past her two eyes and into her third eye. "The next time we talk on the phone, I am going to say: 'Dave said we have a long fight ahead, and it could be a year or two before the trial actually starts.' I'll need you to reply with: 'It's okay. I'll be here for you, no matter how long it takes.'"

I paused, waiting for Vera to get out of her heart and into her head. I prayed she wouldn't overthink the plan and create more problems than already existed. I needed verification that she wouldn't tip off Ron.

"I get it. I'll play my role to a T," Vera replied, knowing I'd never fold.

"We cannot let the DEA know how much we miss each other. It's very important you don't talk about this strategy in your house, with your friends, on your phone, or ever again— for however long it takes. I need you to pretend your life is fine without me, but don't make it obvious—be subtle. Play along with whatever I say on the phone and stay positive. I can win this without a trial."

Ron had been using Vera against me, by separating us, but now I'd use her against him, because I was more determined than ever to win, and I fully trusted Vera could create the illusion we were comfortable being separated.

I lost sight of "why" I wanted to beat Ron, and it seemed to be turning into a primal power game, as I regularly found myself subconsciously comparing my strength and status to Ron's. I think it was because I was so used to winning in life that I refused to lose. My problem was, Ron was used to winning, too. I figured most of his targets usually submitted to him, and with each submission, his confidence in his ability to break people grew. It was a snowball effect that allowed him to continue winning, but I've found there's one way to halt someone's winning streak . . . and that's through persistence. That's how I always did it, because persistence is what helped me unlock my potential. It also provided me with progress, and that's what I was, and that's what we all are—a work in progress.

Jim was willing to help outwit Ron, too, and I explained the game plan during our next visit. I told him I'd be calling him on the phone within a week to ask, "What's the status of getting Dave his check?" When Ron heard this, I knew he'd assume I was gaining strength, and it'd be one more hair he could pull out of his head on account of Eric "Slick" Canori.

29

RESPONSIBILITY

While the other inmates played solitaire, I spent the next three months alone in my cell meditating before each of my planned weekly phone conversations. I made sure not to make any mistakes. Each conversation was nonchalant, precise, and plausible, as I carefully focused my attention on Ron's perspective, planning out all his next moves for him. It was mental warfare, and I'd eventually get Ron to submit, offering a deal I could accept, because I was done playing the odds. I was now playing Ron from a six-by-eight-foot cell.

ARE YOU KIDDING ME? In less than four months, Ron called Jim and said, "All Eric has to do is surrender the rest of his money, and he'll never see another day in jail."

Fuck yeah! My hard work had paid off. Ron knew Jim visited me weekly, and must've thought Jim could persuade me into submitting. I asked Jim how much "the rest of" meant during our next visit, and he replied, "I don't know; he didn't say. Just give him everything you have."

"Everything" was a difficult word for me to grasp. Jim had no idea how much I had, and if Ron thought I was going back to McDonald's to flip patties for $7.25 per hour, he must have been smoking crack. Maybe he'd at least release my legitimate assets back to me. I needed Dave's help with this one, so the following day, I called him and I asked him to set up a meeting for us with Ron, to verify my new option of cooperation. I wanted to hear it from the horse's mouth.

Sure enough, Dave successfully set the meeting up for the following week, at the United States Attorney's Office, in downtown Albany. Part of me felt honored for the invite, since there are only ninety-three U.S. attorneys and 350 assistant U.S. attorneys in the entire United States. I felt like I was getting ready to go on a field trip. I was going to visit one of the most powerful law firms in the world, the United States government—an entity that doesn't negotiate with terrorists, but sometimes with drug dealers. Especially ones like me, who had a lot to offer.

IT WAS June 2011 when Ron and his partner transported me to the meeting. I calculated it had been two years since I'd first crossed paths with Ron, and I could see the snow had melted away since I'd last been outside. Everyone I saw had their sunglasses on, and the trees were in full bloom, and I wasn't focused on being shackled in the back seat of Ron's Chevy Malibu. Instead, I was focused on the things I'd missed, which I'd previously taken for granted: the fresh air, the sun, and the wind brushing across my face from the open front windows. I would've paid Ron a million bucks for a quick detour to Chipotle, but we didn't speak during the transport—even though both our spirits seemed elevated. However, at the end of our fifteen-minute drive, while parking in the back of the U.S. courthouse, Ron did make one statement: "Today's your opportunity to make everything right and get on with your life. Don't fuck it up."

I heard Ron, but I was busy staring at the most intimidating part of the courthouse. The United States Department of Justice emblem, the bald eagle, the bird of prey, the opportunistic feeder . . . the only bird that flies above the clouds when it rains. I wondered who came up with that emblem. It seemed like a good fit, considering the U.S. Department of Justice had close to a ninety-five percent conviction rate.

I was nervous. This was the most important meeting of my life, and it wasn't going to be about what I deserved; it'd be about what I negotiated. I needed to listen carefully, before I said anything.

It was good to see Dave when I arrived in the conference room. His spirits also seemed elevated as he asked Ron for a moment alone with me. Ron obliged, and left us sitting at a six-person conference table, in a small room, tucked toward the back of the U.S. Attorney's Office. There was a lot of clutter around the perimeter of the room, and I assumed there could be any number of recording devices hidden among it, so we used our usual protocol: the whisper.

Dave started with, "Nothing you say or discuss today can be used against you. Pretrial negotiations are inadmissible in court."

That was a relief to hear; I was wondering how this worked.

"I don't have anything to say. I just want to know how much money Ron wants," I whispered into Dave's ear.

My plan was to isolate the investigation by giving Ron my money, in exchange for him not making me set up any of my past connections. If he could agree to that, I'd surrender my war chest, because keeping my word with my team was more important than all my money. My words were the building blocks of my entire existence. They reflected my integrity, built my reputation, and opened countless closed doors for me over the years.

Our conversation was cut short as Ron, his partner, and the prosecuting assistant U.S. attorney entered the room. They swooped in like true eagles. They didn't have any predators; they were the law. The prosecutor was young and strong and wore a well-cut suit, which perfectly complemented his fresh buzz cut. Kennedy had mentioned the prosecutor had recently served as a JAG attorney in Guantanamo Bay, and I could immediately sense his loyalty, duty, and respect for the United States. He seemed like a straight shooter, and as he raised his hand toward me, I raised my cuffed hands for a firm handshake.

We kept the pleasantries brief, and after the prosecutor handed me a bottle of water, Ron popped off my cuffs as we sat down and the prosecutor immediately kicked in with, "Eric, we believe you have eight to nine million hidden. We know about the gold too."

Ouch, that number was higher than I was expecting. And how the fuck did they know I had gold? There were less than three people on earth who knew. Maybe Ron had seen a magazine picture of gold on my Vision Board at home and it was pure speculation. I exhaled deeply and shook my head, conveying the number was too high, he was wasting time, and to try again. But he didn't. He just continued on with, "We want to know everything, including information regarding your dealings with Cora."

"I'm sorry to interrupt, but I think we have a misunderstanding. I was under the impression I didn't have to set anyone up," I said, angry with Ron's bait-and-switch. "I thought this meeting was for matters pertaining to my assets."

I'm not sure if any of them knew Ron had passed a message to me through Jim, saying all he wanted was my money in exchange for my freedom. But I didn't call Ron out, even though my lack of trust in him had just weakened the possibility of making a deal.

"Hold on, can we please have a moment alone?" Dave asked the eagles.

They all exited the room in silence, and our whispering commenced.

"Relax. If they only want one person, that's a good deal. Cora's going down with Missy's information anyway. If you cooperate, you don't have to tell them everything; you just can't lie. Let's hear them out," Dave said, holding my shoulder close, his voice reverberating in my ear.

"What about the money? The number they're asking for is impossible. I can't get it," I lied, calibrating my tactics to Ron's false advertising.

"How much can you get?"

"About two mil."

"Okay, let me do the talking."

The birds of prey came back into the room and settled into their chairs.

"Eric won't testify against Cora, and the amount of money you're requesting is impossible," Dave said.

Ron's face turned red. We all sensed a stalemate approaching, but the prosecutor tried to save the negotiations with, "Eric, how much can you get?"

"I don't know the exact number. Maybe around 2.3 million. It could be a little less; it could be a little more," I replied.

I liked the sound of that number. It felt real, fair, and believable. But Ron's face was getting redder by the second, and we all observed him use his forearm sleeve to wipe sweat from his forehead, before he burst out, "No! No deal! That's not enough."

Ron looked ready to shake my money out of me faster than Mom shook it out of my piggy bank. He was fuming. I think he realized he'd been waiting for something that wasn't going to happen. Fuck, I could relate. I'd spent years feeding my frustrations with my unmet expectations. Actually, my expectations were the root of all my pain in life. Dave could relate too, and that's when he requested a conversation with the prosecutor alone, outside of the room. Ron's partner stayed behind with the two of us, which probably prevented Ron from bouncing my head off the table like Daffy Duck.

When Dave came back into the room, he asked to speak with me alone. It seemed he'd converted some bad news into good news. I was hopeful, because at this point, hope was the only thing I had.

Once the eagles left the room, Dave said he'd convinced the prosecutor to agree to a forfeiture totaling $4,750,000. This figure included the $2,700,000 they'd already confiscated from me, and an additional $2,050,000 I'd have to come up with. The number seemed reasonable, but we couldn't get the prosecutor to budge on Cora, and he only gave us twenty-four hours to reach a decision. Hence, I immediately felt pressure. I could deal with it, though, but to fix it I needed to spend time alone. And that's exactly what I was going to do before I replied to the prosecutor.

AFTER RON DELIVERED me back to jail, I spent the night in my cell mulling over the ramifications of pleading guilty to the marijuana indictment. I liked that the money laundering charge would disappear, I liked that I'd still have enough money left for Vera to buy heirloom vegetables at the farmers market for life, and I liked that my associates wouldn't go down with me. Except Cora. She was the problem I couldn't solve, the problem I didn't create, and the problem I'd have to either pay or not pay for. I couldn't get Dave's last words to stop echoing in my head, "Cora's going down with or without your information. So if you want to see the light of day again, take the deal."

Cora created a sticky situation for me. Her greed had put her in Ron's crosshairs, and her name would never have come up if she'd listened to me. Her rush to the top had put my life in jeopardy, and as I contemplated all my options, they kept leading back to: Can I trust Cora? She bait-and-switched me twice, she talked to Missy behind my back, and I only knew of her from about six deals over a one-year period. If I go to trial, will she testify against me once Ron scoops her up? I was in a tough spot. I didn't know if she would.

That night in my cell, I practiced Charles Haanel's lessons to help me find the answer to my question. I meditated. I needed to know if Cora would testify against me. I needed to know if she lived a truthful life, within the natural laws of the universe. The universe in which everything moves in circular patterns, and the universe in which everything is connected to everything else. A place where nothing happens by chance, but where every action has a reaction; hence, we reap what we sow.

So I asked myself, what does Cora sow? Because I'd sown good and I'd sown bad, and I continued to receive tests and lessons. Tests that challenged me to see how true I could remain to my heart while solving problems. A heart I guarded closely, and a heart where I was learning to find my answers. And the deeper I looked into my heart, the clearer I saw Cora going down with Missy's information, and then helping Ron hang me if I went to trial. So, since I wasn't ready to do ten-plus years by being faithful to someone who'd be unfaithful to me, I woke the next morning and pulled my trigger first.

"Dave, it's Eric. If it's just Cora and no one else, let's do the deal," I said over the inmate phone system.

"Good choice, my friend. You'll be happy to know, I also

convinced them to preserve your right to appeal one ambivalent aspect of your case," Dave replied.

Dave was a genius. Even though I'd be pleading guilty to conspiring to distribute a schedule one substance, Dave structured the deal to make sure we could argue the invalidity of my case in the Second Circuit, due to a de facto rescheduling of marijuana in the Controlled Substance Act. Meaning, marijuana could no longer be considered a schedule one substance, because in October 2009, Deputy Attorney General David Ogden had released a memo directing federal prosecutors to allow state regulation of commercial activity in medical marijuana. The state regulations undermined and nullified federal law, which is supposed to be the supreme law of the land. If Dave could win this argument, my case would make history in solving a "constitutional crisis," and my guilty plea would be overturned. There was also a chance my seized cash would be returned to me, so I could say, "Look, Mom, it all started with a dream."

IT ONLY TOOK a few days for the prosecutor and Dave to draft up the particulars of my plea agreement. Ron then brought me back to the courthouse for my signature and to stand before Judge Sharpe, for my guilty plea. At the courthouse, I sat with Dave and perused the agreement one final time. It looked fair, stating only what Missy knew and had told them about my operation: Eric Canori distributed marijuana domestically for a year and a half. There were no mentions of my Canadian export business, which spanned ten-plus years, or the fact that I had sold over $300 million worth of grass by age twenty-nine. It felt like a slap on the wrist, but the forfeiture was going to sting.

"I'll get you a pen," Ron said, seeing me ready to sign.

"You're going to need to get a shovel, too," I replied, looking up at him from the signature line.

"What do you mean?" Ron asked, weighing every word in our first semi-cordial conversation.

"I can surrender the full two million today, in gold, but it's buried in the ground."

"Where?"

"In my Mom's backyard."

Ron wasn't surprised. He just shook his head and immediately called Jim's cell phone, requesting permission to enter his property for the dig. I wondered who'd do the digging, because I was still in shackles, Dave had a suit on, and Ron was dressed for a tropical vacation. Thankfully, Dave was coming with us to photograph the dig, just in case Ron decided to flee to Tahiti with my precious metals. Part of me could envision him sipping mojitos there while saying, "Cheers, to everyone working hard on their dreams."

Within thirty minutes, Ron had assembled more than twenty DEA and ATF agents, armed with assault rifles, bulletproof vests, and walkie-talkie headsets, to escort us to the dig. The convoy stormed up the highway, single file, at around 90 mph in the fast lane. Ron must have assumed there was a slight possibility I was leading him into an ambush, so I could escape to Tahiti without him. I suppose if it had been a movie, I could've had a team waiting for me with more firepower than them, keys to my shackles, and an outfit to replace my yellow jumpsuit. Then I could've vanished. But I wasn't about to cop out. I needed closure, because like Mom always said, "Take responsibility for your actions. It shows you're reliable."

A mile from Mom's house, Ron's entire squad regrouped in a public parking lot. They had a brief meeting, tested their headsets, then half of them fanned out to form a secure perimeter around Mom's small residential neighborhood. When we pulled up to Mom's with the other half of Ron's squad, no one was home. Jim must've told Mom to leave the house so she wouldn't have nightmares.

With Ron's crew hot on my heels, I led him into the backyard. It felt good to finally touch the earth after living in concrete for the last four months. It was a priceless vacation from the fluorescent lights, and as I soaked up the eighty degrees and clear skies, I could smell the vegetation around us. I couldn't wait to be back on the lake with Vera.

"Right here," I said, stopping and standing above my cache, kicking the toe of my orange inmate-issued shoe into the loose gravel.

"How deep?" Ron asked.

"Three feet."

It was a spectacle to watch Ron commence the groundbreaking ceremony with the rusty pointed blade of his shovel. The only things missing were the hardhats, a PA system, and a speech. There was already a small crowd of DEA and IRS agents from the guest list to make sure everything went kosher.

After Ron had dug a little over three feet, still hitting rocks, he looked up toward me, dripping sweat like a pig. I could tell he was questioning my credibility and I started to wonder if someone had robbed me. He should've reached the toolbox by now, I thought, remaining seated on the lawn as two armed guards hovered over me. I could sense Ron's anxiety setting in, along with mine.

"Can I get up and take a look, please?" I asked the guards.

Ron nodded to them, allowing me to come peer into the hole.

I saw one very large rock where Ron had stopped, and recognized its shape immediately, remembering I'd placed it over the toolbox as a final deterrent. "Oh yeah, it's just under that rock," I said.

That's when I saw the first glimpse of victory cross Ron's eyes. And once I heard the hollow sound from the tip of his shovel hit the toolbox, my relief set in, as I was now one step closer to something priceless—freedom.

Soon after, I witnessed Ron feverishly lift the hundred-pound box out of the hole, place it on Mom's lawn, open it, and lay out the one-kilogram gold bars in a neat line. They twinkled under the summer sun, as the IRS, DEA, and Dave photographed them. It was my first time being acknowledged for my accomplishments at a high-profile ceremony. And within minutes, Dave received a call from the prosecutor, congratulating us for most likely making history as the fastest defendant to ever pay their judgment in full. Actually, there was $300,000 more than I owed. If only Mom was home, she could've held a spotlight on my gold medal ceremony, as if I was in the Olympics.

I don't like to brag. I mostly live in the periphery, but there still remained a part of me that wanted to hear, "Good job, Eric, you did it," because it was always difficult for me to get out of my head: "Eric, you're never going to make it." But no, I did "make it," monetarily at least, and this was my day and I wanted to be praised for my achievement.

Everyone wants to be praised for their achievements. It's biological. It's about being accepted by our tribes, because we all live in some sort of tribe, and we all subliminally know we're being monitored one way or another by its members. I see examples of this every day. All I have to do is open up my social media and look at those who use it to promote themselves: *Look at me! I did it! Do you accept me?* Fuck yeah, I accept you! Let's hang, I'm sitting here alone, scrolling.

30

HOODWINKED

R on remained calm while driving me back to jail after the dig, not saying anything except, "Nice job. It's a good start."

Fucking prick, I thought. He'd hoodwinked me again. I knew he couldn't be trusted. It seemed he wanted more money before he'd recommend to the court I was no longer a flight risk and that my bail be set. I couldn't believe it, but I did. Ron was turning out to be a real gold digger, one I couldn't shake. Saying I was bankrupt wouldn't work with him.

I COULDN'T FALL asleep in my cell that night, knowing in the morning I'd have to brief Ron on my illicit activities, and somehow confirm my interactions with Cora, without implicating anyone else in my organization. I turned to Charles Haanel once again, seeking a solution to my problem. I could see the dice were loaded in Ron's favor. I could clearly see him prying for information that could lead him to more money, and he had one thing he was holding over my head to do it—I still hadn't been sentenced. I had pleaded guilty, but Judge Sharpe still needed to sentence me based on my level of cooperation with Ron, and I only saw two options for cooperation. I could give up people I knew that had money, or give up the rest of my gold.

"So TELL me everything about your business, from the very beginning," Ron said, kicking off my proffer session the following morning at his headquarters.

Ron's crew hadn't even taken their first sip of coffee, and I sensed he was getting ready to hunt outside the parameters of our agreement, just as I'd suspected he would.

Ron was the only one without a notepad this time. The prosecutor, Dave, the three DEA agents, and an IRS agent all had pens in hand with blank notepads open. I was facing the biggest challenge of my life. I had to make this a win-win deal for my organization and the government, without committing perjury. I had a plan, though. In order to remain perjury-free, I'd play stupid, talk slow, draw out the session, exhaust Ron, and flood him with old, useless information from my past that would result in dead-end leads. I'd draw things out until he'd ask the one question I suspected he was waiting to sneak in, and a question that he shouldn't have asked, according to our agreement.

"So tell me about the gold. How much did you buy?" Ron eventually inquired. And there it was, his most valuable question, the one I was waiting for, and the one I'd leverage to save my associates.

"I'm not sure . . . a lot," I replied.

Everyone in the room immediately took their eyes off their notepads and lasered in on me. Nothing was more valuable to them than the keys to Fort Knox.

"How much is 'a lot'?" Ron probed.

"I don't remember exactly."

The entire room fluttered, notepads were moving, eyes were glaring, hearts were racing, and I started envisioning Ron's clasped hands tightening around my neck as Dave came to my rescue with, "Can I please have a moment with my client, alone?"

They obliged, and all stepped out of the room.

"Why did you say 'a lot'?" Dave whispered.

"We made a deal to only give Cora, and now Ron's digging for other people. I didn't sign for this."

Ron interrupted us, marching back into the small room with his army. Everyone seemed frustrated and there was a quick mutual understanding that we were at a stalemate.

My plan had worked precisely. I had alerted Ron I had more gold, knowing he couldn't access it without my cooperation, because I'd already fulfilled my end of our agreement. I'd surrendered five million, and I'd told him what I did with Cora. He had no recourse.

I'm not stupid. I had intentionally soured the meeting by saying "a lot." I could've forgotten I had more gold and instead said, "I don't recall." But I wanted Ron to know there was more, so he'd beg for it, with fair terms, and leave my associates alone. I wasn't giving him another flake of gold until I was reassured he would no longer try to use me as his lackey to set people up. My cooperation would be in the form of voluntarily surrendering the map to the rest of my buried treasure. In exchange, I wanted reassurance that Judge Sharpe would be notified of my substantial cooperation prior to my sentencing. This was the only way I'd voluntarily surrender the rest of my treasure.

Of course I cheated the system by selling weed, but I wasn't about to let Ron use the system to cheat me.

Ron looked like he wanted to hold his Glock to my head, but all he could do was place the cuffs back on me and deliver me back to jail. The prosecutor remained calm and stated we would resume talks the following day, but I knew that wasn't going to happen, because I was done being bait for Ron's fishing expedition. He needed time to understand the practices of fair trade. He was cheating, probably for the same reason other people cheat . . . because they think others are cheating, and they don't want to be left behind. That's partially why I did it.

31

ALONE

I was at an impasse with Ron. He wanted me to assist him in more ways than we had agreed upon, and I wouldn't. So my only option was to stand alone in my cell for what was right, and that's what I did, as the days turned to night and the nights turned to day. I did have a familiar plan, though. I'd continue communicating with Ron through my phone conversations with Jim and Vera, as he listened in closely, while I'd create calculated phrases suggesting I was done assisting him, that he couldn't be trusted, and that I'd rather rot in jail than help him. I'd make sure he knew the only way I'd surrender the rest of the gold was if I was guaranteed freedom and was done with the proffer session.

AFTER A COUPLE WEEKS HAD PASSED, Ron still wouldn't budge, and I started losing all hope. I was out of options, too. I started thinking it was going to be years before I could go home.

I was only thirty-two, and I looked pathetic lying alone on my cell bed in the fetal position, curled up questioning my motives in life, other people's motives, and everything I thought was true. I felt like I was at an ayahuasca ceremony. I was face to face with my deepest fears. I could see how I had become a puppet, doing the same things over and over, for other people's approval. I could see how I'd lost my soul, always trying to keep up. Actually, I had sold my soul. My life was no longer about making money for food and shelter . . . my millions were being stacked to be noticed. To be accepted. To be loved. To be enough for one woman. To financially support one woman, so she wouldn't complain about lack of money or leave me for a man with more money.

My entire existence was fear based. What an exhausting way to live, but at the opposite end of fear, I could see love. I could almost feel it. It felt like something I'd never fully experienced. Probably because I'd lived in fear for most of my life. I'd lived in fear of not having enough money. Why? Because without money, who was I? Just a lonely kid in the lunchroom who no one noticed. Just a loser. I hated being called a loser. I could've won, if we all had an equal start. That's why I liked playing Monopoly, because each player started with the same amount of cash. There was no need to break the law in that game.

As I curled up tighter, I thought about all the kids who have unstable home environments. The kids who don't get a fair and equal start. The kids who get locked in cages. The kids who sleep on dirt floors. The kids who have to steal to eat. The ones who have to sell drugs to eat. The ones who end up in prison. The ones who've had it much worse than me. And right then, I started to realize I didn't have it anywhere nearly as bad as some kids. In fact, I had a lot to be grateful for, even Mom and Jim. I would've never experienced everything I had without them. They'd taught me priceless lessons. They pushed me to be better. And even though I didn't agree with all their methods, who was to say mine were right? I was still trying to figure out life every day.

"ERIC, I have some good news! I just spoke with Ron. He reassured me all you have to do is give him the rest of your gold and you can get on with your life. He said you're smart enough to make more money elsewhere," Dave said over the inmate phone line.

My jaw dropped; I was back on track. On top of it, it was a week before Independence Day, my favorite time of the year to cut loose. I appreciated Ron's compliment, too. Maybe we were on our way to letting bygones be bygones.

"This is good to hear," I replied calmly, careful not to jinx it. "Does Ron know I'm not setting anyone up, and that I'm done giving him information about my past?" I asked.

"Yeah, he just wants the gold. That'll be considered significant cooperation. Also, the prosecutor and I will make Judge Sharpe aware of your substantial cooperation."

"How can we trust them? Can we get it in writing?" I asked.

"No, I can't get it in writing. You can't buy your way out of jail, but I trust Ron now. Either way, I don't think we have a better option at this point. Tim also recommends you take the deal, if you ever want to see the light of day."

I felt a little uneasy giving Ron a second chance, but I didn't think he wanted to be known as a guy who couldn't be trusted. Also, I was missing Vera more than ever, and I couldn't see her waiting for me much longer. Plus, doing the deal meant I'd only be losing money, not my loyalty to others. And Ron was right; I could make the money back because making money was never as difficult as being broke. It just required time and sacrifices. It was about self-control and avoiding temptations. And I'd become a master at avoiding temptations, because I was at a

point in life where I could immediately assess whether something would scatter or center me, which was another key to my
success.

Once I told Dave I'd surrender the rest of the gold, Ron
didn't waste a minute retrieving me from jail to take him on
another dig. Again, I wore shackles and led twenty DEA/ATF
agents, armed with AR-15s, into the woods of Saratoga, as a
steady rain fell, and I directed them to two spots: one with a
chest containing $5,000,000 in gold bars, and a second with a
chest containing $1,500,000 in gold bars. Ron dug up the smaller
chest first; we then made our way to the larger one, which was
located about one hundred paces north of the smaller one.
When Ron's shovel hit the last cache, about three feet down, he
had a huge smile on his face and I had one to match. I'd just
bought my ticket to Vera.

It took four guys to lift my 230-pound-plus war chest out of
the earth, and Special Agent Ronald Arp was a fucking hero.
Between the weed, gold, and cash seized at my houses, Ron had
squeezed over $12.5 million out of me, and finally spoke his first
cordial words to me.

"You know this is just business, right? You could've saved
yourself a lot of money if you'd worked with me in the beginning," Ron said, as we followed the DEA/ATF agents out of the
woods carrying my war chests.

I didn't bother to explain myself, but there was no way I
could've lived with myself if I had worked for him. He would
have had me pose as a supplier and continue selling weed, so he
could have seized my associates' money. This is what's known as
a reverse sting, and it's completely legal, even though juries have
a hard time believing in them. So I simply nodded and replied
with, "Can you order us some Chipotle?" And that's exactly what
he did.

My deal with Ron was finally revolving around long-term

mutual gain, rather than inflexible demands. Of course our give-and-take approach was drawn out over two years, but sometimes that's what cooperation is about. Creating win-win deals. Giving as much as you take. Yeah sure, people tell me I shouldn't have given up the gold, but the gold wasn't a loss—it was the greatest lesson of my life. Ron pushed me out of the person I'd been, and into the person I was becoming. A person who was learning to be happy with where they were—rather than where they wanted to be. A person who was finding his center. A person who recognized that every event is a combination of good and bad, and wasn't allowing that to affect his peace of mind.

I was learning to go with the flow. Sure, I still had big goals and big dreams, but I wasn't as attached to them as I had been in the past, because attachment to the future is what had me trapped for years on end.

AFTER RON CALLED someone to fetch us Chipotle, we headed back to the DEA headquarters to eat and tally the gold bars in his associate's and Dave's presence. It was a beautiful sight. It was my last bargaining chip to avoid punishment. It was the type of event you read about in Roman history books, and once Ron was satisfied, he promptly called the prosecutor and notified him of my outstanding cooperation and recommended I be released from custody.

Sure enough, the following day Judge Sharpe set my bail at $1 million, and Mom and Jim unfailingly came to my rescue, and once again put up their house. Soon after, Dave recommended I remain on bail for as long as possible to let the dust settle before I faced Judge Sharpe for sentencing.

I waited for several months, as Dave kept pushing the sentencing off. I assumed I'd get "time served" the longer I waited, but the waiting began creating friction between Vera and I. She was getting bored of waiting and bored of our simple life. She wanted to have "fun." She wanted to do more things that only money could buy, and with her wants came stress. Stress I experienced from the pressure of thinking I had to buy things for "us." And with her unmet expectations, I began feeling I was lacking as a provider, and sensed it was just a matter of time before her cravings spiraled out of control. Cravings that I wouldn't be able to fulfill, and cravings that wouldn't fulfill me.

There was no way I was going to get a job to buy a bunch of shit that would end up in a landfill before I was in my grave. We didn't need new coats anyway. The ones we had from the prior winter were barely used. Plus, I didn't care what the neighbors thought. They bought their ski jackets with a credit card, and I could see that their debt owned them by the blue rings under their eyes. I didn't want to be them, so much so that I split up with Vera, as I mentally prepared to stand before Sharpe, knowing he had the authority to sentence me however he deemed fit.

"GOOD MORNING, YOUR HONOR," I replied to Judge Sharpe's opening of the federal courtroom. I was standing up straight, in a tailored navy blue suit, showing my utmost respect.

"All right. We're here for the purposes of sentencing. I've reviewed the pre-sentence report and both parties' submissions," Sharpe stated.

Fortunately, Dave and the prosecutor had briefed the court of my exceptional cooperation several weeks prior, both acknowledging I'd voluntarily surrendered all the proceeds from my criminal activity. In addition, Sharpe gave me the opportunity to speak and represent myself in the courtroom.

And when I spoke, I began explaining how I'd lost sight of my choices, and that I had other talents to offer society if given a second chance. That's when Sharpe cut me off and said, "Money, right?"

"Pardon me?" I replied.

"You did it for the easy money, right?"

"It was—" I began to explain, but Sharpe interrupted again with a pep talk about crime, and when he allowed me to resume speaking, I was too embarrassed to get into the entire truth of my motives in a public courtroom. So I simply said, "It started with me trying to make a few bucks to get a peaceful meal." I didn't explain much more, and I didn't think Sharpe would relate with my truth even if I did. Plus, it would've been too generic for a criminal setting, because most criminals have difficult childhoods. It's been studied and proven.

"Eric, my hands are significantly tied with this. Yes, I have the ability to sentence you below the mandatory minimum, but my work is monitored, so I have to be fair across the board. Therefore the sentence I impose is—thirty months," Sharpe stated.

I didn't hear what he said after that. All I could hear was "thirty months" echoing in my head, but I wasn't sure if I'd heard Sharpe correctly, so I looked over to Dave. He was shocked, too, and with a nod, he verified I'd heard correctly.

I was speechless. Missy had already received time served, Rob had received time served, and the money I voluntarily surrendered was in the process of being distributed to the thirty-three law enforcement agencies that had assisted Ron in taking me down. Cora had received a sixty-month sentence, but that's because she didn't play her cards right. It was my understanding she had cooperated with Ron for a few months after her arrest, but later refused to cooperate, as Ron pushed her to work harder. She also didn't forfeit her million-dollar house on the beach in Central America. She kept it and did her time, which I respected.

News of my prison sentence was difficult to accept, but it started humbling me. I began noticing how many insecurities I'd forged in my youth, and all the shit I did over the years to cover them with money. I began acknowledging that I'm not better than anyone else, and the only way I could survive is in a tribe. I couldn't just move away to some desolate island with my money, a woman, and hidden pain. No, I needed to stay present and become grateful for every good and bad experience I'd ever had. I needed to replace my pain with compassion. Specifically, compassion for others. I needed to realize that I am just a speck in the universe and that everyone has had hidden pain at one time or another. And I mean everyone, because I've found many people hide their pain out of fear and shame. They don't want to be judged as "weak." I think they're the ones who were taught to "just get over it." And there definitely was something I needed to get over. Myself. I needed to get over myself and count my blessings, not my problems. Besides, life is full of problems. Everyone has them. They help us learn. Without them, there's no way to grow.

THANKFULLY, Judge Sharpe gave me six weeks to self-surrender to prison. The irony was, he scheduled me to surrender at 2 p.m. on my birthday. I didn't care, though, because life doesn't revolve around birthdays. It revolves around the sun. What I did care about was when Ron called me out of the blue to share his condolences over my unexpected sentence. He started the call off with, "Colorado shouldn't be selling weed, while you're going to prison for it."

I chuckled, and Ron paused, adding that he'd just been discharged from Dana-Farber Cancer Institute, after recently being diagnosed with colon cancer and having an emergency surgery. I could tell by the grogginess in his voice he was on some heavy pain meds, and when he jokingly asked me for a joint to kill the pain, I actually felt sorry for him. I wished no harm upon him. He even asked me to build his family a trout pond, but I reminded him I'd be away for some time. That's when he surprised me with, "Eric, with the way I work, you'll be out in a year." Which followed with him in a roundabout way of telling me if I cooperated more, he'd recommend to the court that I be released from prison early.

But Ron didn't need me to cooperate. His days were numbered. He was just searching for any legit way to give me a going-away present, before he passed on. I think it was his way of thanking me for making him a hero. After all, we now had an unspoken code of honor and respect—I think because he had heard me on the mics and wires for close to two years, and probably knew me better than I knew myself.

As it turned out, I did have something to give Ron. I'd recently been following news of an arrest and weed case involving Streets, and knew my chances of ever getting my money from him was looking grim. Hence, I decided this was the perfect time to clear up the $160,000 he'd stolen from me. Furnishing Ron with some vague information about Streets would zero out his remaining balance with me, and be my backup plan in case Dave couldn't overturn my guilty plea in the Second Circuit.

Of course, I knew there was already enough evidence to hang Streets without me, and that my information would be useless, but Ron insinuated he'd somehow use it to my advantage.

This was another key to my success . . . I was always ready when opportunities came my way. I could easily spot them, assess them, and determine how to use them. My opportunities were rarely lost. I didn't let things slip by me. Mostly because my external environment was simple and clean. It was organized. My desk was, my closet was, my truck was, and my mind was. I didn't lose things amongst clutter. The only thing I ever lost was my soul.

PATIENCE

I t was January 8, 2013, and Jim and I were exchanging our last words over a cigar on my birthday, before I surrendered myself to the Federal Bureau of Prisons. We were sitting in Jim's Kia Sportage, in a parking lot, facing the building I'd be entering within the hour. The facility looked well-maintained from our vantage point. It was said to house mobsters, white-collar criminals, sex offenders, and drug dealers. I also heard George Jung had recently been transferred out of there. He was the drug smuggler whose story was portrayed in the movie *Blow*, starring Johnny Depp.

As I puffed my cigar, I wondered what other notable criminals were locked in there. The prison was called Federal Medical Center Devens, located in north-central Massachusetts. It housed over one thousand inmates, mostly long-term medical and mental health inmates. I was there for the second-degree burns I'd sustained a few months earlier, across my limbs, when lighting a brush pile using gasoline. It was a careless mistake, but after being airlifted to an ICU for a ten-day stay, my wounds were finally healing quickly on their own, and I didn't need further medical attention. I was placed there anyway, because if by chance my wounds worsened, I needed to be near proper care.

I think it's fair to say my reckless lifestyle was beyond embarrassing by now, but Jim's words grounded me as he relit the foot of his cigar.

"Eric, you're built from every mistake you've made. Everyone is."

I paused in the passenger seat, gazing through the chain-link fence, topped with layers of razor wire, and reflected on my mistakes.

"My biggest mistake was letting the wrong people slip into my circle," I eventually replied.

Jim nodded, as he exhaled a thick plume of smoke out his window. He then looked back toward me and said, "Everyone comes into our lives for a reason. Some just to teach us how to let go."

I rolled my cigar between my fingertips and thought about all the people I had let into my circle. Specifically, the ones who had weakened me and the ones who had drained me. Which was true on countless occasions, because I've found there are only two possible ways you can feel after you hang out with anyone in this world: charged or drained. And I had definitely felt drained after associating with certain people in my circle, and whenever I felt drained, that's when I made all my mistakes in life. I think this is when everyone does.

Jim taught me a lot, and what I really wanted to do was ask him . . . why? Why did you smack me around so much? Part of me wanted to hear his answer, but the other part didn't want to create uneasy feelings before our farewell. Plus, I already knew why. He was simply short-fused due to lack of rest. He was always trying to keep up with the demands in life, while all he really wanted to do was live in peace and later have his ashes spread across the Adirondacks. He said that once, but he was

caught up in the grind just like me. *More, more, more,* with little
time to think about the cause and effects of our actions.

Regardless, I respect Jim—he'd take a bullet for me. I grew
respect for Mom, too. She taught me a lot. She always wanted
the best for me. I imagine most of her values stem from her
parents, who were in the military and who were forced to live in
fear as the Germans bombed their home city, Warsaw, during
World War II. Her parents had to hide in random dusty base-
ments as debris fell, while they lost several family members to
bullets and grenades. Luckily, her parents eventually escaped
and immigrated to America, in the hopes of greater economic
opportunities. And when they arrived stateside unscathed, they
danced and partied every weekend for years in celebration. I
think that's where Mom learned to live for the weekends. I also
think those weekend parties are what weakened her tolerance
for my behavior.

I think this, because I've found that people who party hard
every weekend with their friends usually have turbulent weekdays at home with the ones they love. I know this because I've
spent years processing how weekend choices affect weekday
moods. I hated that roller coaster, and it's taken me a long time
to understand how important it is to lay low on some weekends.
In fact, it's necessary. And again, it comes back to balance, and
balance isn't something you find; it's something you create.

ISOLATION

When an inmate enters prison for the first time, they're usually sent to solitary confinement, also known as "the hole." It's basically a secluded jail within a prison, designed for disruptive inmates who pose a security risk to other inmates and prison staff. It's also where I was escorted after Jim and I parted ways with a hug. I didn't know how long I'd be in the hole; I only knew it was part of the waiting process while prison officials classified my security level, based on my risk to the world.

The hole was a tiny cell, behind a thick steel door, with a steel bed, a steel toilet, a steel sink, and a steel shower that had one temperature: scalding. It was also where I stayed alone for twenty-three hours each day. I could still hear inmates in the neighboring cells, but the only time I saw their faces was when the guards escorted me down the concrete hallway, in shackles, to and from recreation, where I was allowed to spend one hour per day, in a fifteen-by-twenty-foot steel cage, surrounded by tall concrete walls with a view of the sky . . . if I tilted my head back far enough. The inmates would watch as I passed their tiny windows, probably wondering about the nature of my crime, as

I often wondered about the nature of theirs and how many years they'd be calling prison home.

By my sixth day in the hole, a new inmate had arrived in the cell across the fluorescent-lit hallway from me, and as I peeked out the twelve-inch window of my cell door, I could see his face pressed against his glass window. He looked calm, intelligent, and about twenty years my senior. I wanted to ask him questions, but I remained silent, hoping he'd break the ice.

Sure enough, the following day he shouted through the two-inch crack at the base of his door, "What are you in for?"

I got down on my hands and knees, with my face near the crack at the bottom of my door, and shouted: "Weed! How about you?"

"Bank robbery."

"That'll do it," I replied.

I wanted to ask more questions, but I didn't. Instead, I just waited for him to talk. And sure enough, less than a minute later, he asked, "Is this your first time down?"

"Yeah, you?"

"My second and last. I've already been down for five years . . . only three more to go before I can get home to the wifey, if she's still there," he laughed.

I laughed back.

"You got a wife back home?" he asked.

"Nah. I haven't found the one yet," I answered.

He chuckled, and said, "It's not about finding the one, kid— it's about becoming the one."

I didn't know how to respond, so I slowly pulled my face away from the crack below my door and thought about "becoming the one."

Indeed, I was locked in a place with restricted access to

sunlight, and a place where time and perception became distorted, but this was a privilege of a lifetime. It was a window of downtime to reinvent myself. It was a time when I could become a better me, for a better woman, and anyone around me. So I stood up, took one step to the left, leaned on my sink, and calmly stared into the tiny mirror attached to the concrete wall, as an extreme amount of determination ran through me. Perched there, I could see the one person and the only person who could change my life for the better. It was me, and I no longer wanted to be better than anyone else; I just wanted to be better than I used to be.

In one fluid motion, I pushed myself back from the mirror, sat on the edge of my bed, with my elbows on my knees, clasping my hands, and made a pact with myself. A pact to stop focusing on the hurtful things that had been done to me, but instead to focus on all the things that I could do right for others. Things that would add value to others' lives. And the first step to helping others was to fix myself, from the inside out. And in order to do that, I needed to be at peace. I knew this because all the books on Vera's bookshelf had one common message: inner peace is the key to strength and power.

So that was it; having inner peace would be the first step to becoming "the one." Not only that, it'd be the best way to handle all my daily affairs. It'd be the best way to deal with life. There was no more time to spend another day at war with myself, and I was done counting the days with penciled tally marks on my cell wall. Starting in the morning, I'd make the days count.

THE NEXT MORNING, I woke at 6 a.m. for my new routine of complete awareness in order to become the one. I started with meditation. Vera taught me this. She said meditation is the best route to inner transformation. She said it would help me stay focused. She said it would help me gain new perspectives on stressful situations. So as I sat on the edge of my bed, I focused on deep abdominal breathing.

I felt calm, and the deeper I breathed, the stronger I felt. I felt peace. I felt like I was at the place where I needed to start every day. I no longer wanted to rush out the door in the morning and let society pound me in whichever direction it wanted to. I was done with that lifestyle, and I was done having a soul-crushing profession, just to create a life that looked good on the outside. That would only entertain my neighbors, and I didn't have time for that. What I had time for was to create a life that felt good on the inside. A life I could live with, because when I eventually stepped back into freedom, I wanted my internal world to be so strong that I'd never have to blame my outer world for anything again.

Next, breakfast was served through a tray slot in my steel door. I took the time to properly chew each bite, because Vera taught me that chewing allows for the absorption of more nutrients; hence, more power. I also made sure to avoid all sugary and processed foods on the tray, because I ate from farms, not factories.

Next, I did a few calisthenic exercises to blow off negative energy and to balance my emotions. Exercising cleared my mind so I could think about how I was going to find my place in the world and add value to it. I wanted to help people live in harmony with nature, and the only way to do that was to make sure I was. So that's exactly what I started doing—performing my daily tasks around my circadian rhythm. A rhythm that I found, and a rhythm that I live with, because when I prioritize my daily routine around the rise and fall of my energy levels, my days run much smoother. This was another key to my success. It may be one of the most important, because I've found whenever I live out of touch with my primal rhythm, I burn out. It's taken me a while to understand this, but I've finally learned that our biological rhythms are constantly trying to mimic those of the universe, and I no longer fight that synchronicity. I roll with it. The seasonal rhythms, the tidal rhythms, the pulse of the earth . . . they're the most real thing there is. So when I closed my eyes, I felt that shit and it strengthened me. I no longer needed to eat four grams of mushrooms to feel this. The only reason I had in the past was because I was lost.

AFTER I SPENT ABOUT two weeks in the hole working on myself, with the same daily routine, I was transferred to an adjacent minimum security satellite camp. The camp was located just outside the main prison walls, and housed about 120 inmates in a small, steel warehouse with a bunch of side-by-side cubicles, each containing one steel bunk bed and two steel gym lockers. Each six-by-eight-foot, open-air cubicle was home to two nonviolent inmates, who provided labor to the prison at a pay rate of anywhere from eleven cents up to $1.80 per hour.

My job paid eleven cents per hour and consisted of mopping floors, cleaning bathrooms, and wiping down tables. I was able to work at my own pace, collect my thoughts, and continue my mission of becoming the one. The mission was about peeling back my layers, like an onion, so I could reveal my epicenter— my true self—the total sum of all my experiences to date.

I can't believe how many layers I wore, but everyone wears them. The layers are like masks covering our souls, and at one point I had on so many masks that I didn't even know who I was. I subconsciously identified myself by what watch I wore, what shoes I wore, what jacket I wore, who I knew . . . fuck, I wore a lot of masks, but thankfully I shed a lot, too. I stopped wearing my shiny watch, I stopped talking about my accomplishments, and I had gotten rid of ninety percent of my pain. I think I was off to a good start. I was finding the best version of myself, from the inside out. The authentic version, not the version I thought I ought to be to please others.

I think some people call this minimalism, but I call it freedom. Freedom from things that weighed me down. Regardless of what it's called, all I knew was that the fewer things I had between me and nature, the more I got to feel in life, and my life was based on feelings. Feelings are how I experienced life, and I felt more when I had less on and around me. I no longer needed designer labels and drugs to feel good. I felt good by slowly removing things from my life, rather than adding things. Less was more. Sure, I still owned things. I liked things that made me feel good, some of which were expensive. The key was, I wasn't attached to what I owned, and I no longer identified myself by what I owned. I identified myself by where I was, and where I wanted to go.

THE GROUNDS WERE SURPRISINGLY scenic outside our warehouse —lots of green grass, pine trees, and a dirt walking track next to a cemetery, which reminded me to be thankful to be alive.

I had a small group of guys I spent time with at camp. One was a former mayor in for overseas wire fraud in Greece, and two others who were in for tax evasion. I didn't associate with any former drug dealers. Actually, I spent most of my time alone doing push-ups and reading books—ones that Mom mailed to me, which ranged from how to grill a meal to how to follow your heart.

Mom supported me like a champ, and I felt loved. Anytime I called her, she said she wanted to see me, which she did, as she and Jim made the seven-hour drive to visit me multiple times. The visits lasted about four hours, and mostly encompassed surface conversations, because I knew it made them uncomfortable to talk about the past. Particularly my childhood, so I didn't go there. Instead, I enjoyed the little time we had together, remained grateful for their support, and most importantly remained patient. Why? Because timing is everything.

Sure, there was a lot I wanted to discuss with them about my upbringing, but they weren't ready, and I wasn't ready. I knew so, because I understood timing, which is simply about having good intuition as to when to make your move. Plus, like I said before, my childhood wasn't as traumatizing as those who have faced sexual abuse, abandonment, extreme poverty, or death of a loved one—like Mom had, at age ten, when she lost her father to heart complications. The bottom line is, we all have some degree of trauma. The key is to recognize it sooner than later. This is how you start the healing process. You have to be patient, though, because there isn't a correct timetable for healing. Fuck, I still am healing, but I feel better than ever.

I think my healing process began when Mom was there for me while I was in prison. It wasn't just her visits, but also her letters, which she wrote plenty of, and I wrote plenty back. The letters weren't deep, but they were a pleasure to receive and send. They contained words like *Dear, I miss you, I hope all is well,* and *Love.* We were building a healthy relationship that felt right. We were accepting each other for who we were. Our relationship was no longer about trying to change each other, and she no longer had to tell me right from wrong. She just wanted to spend time with me before it was too late. She said, "We might not get another chance."

Mom was right. None of us know if tomorrow will come. Chances are good that it will, but we don't know what it will bring. For me it's been handcuffs and a couple airlifts to the ICU, which changed my life forever, but for others, it could be something as common as a heart attack or cancer. I speak from experience, because on my second helicopter trip to the ICU, after my ski accident, I thought my life was over. For a minute, on the gurney I could see all the faces of my loved ones rapidly flash between the spinning blades above me. I wanted to say, "Thank you. I love you," but no one was there. That was hard. Not even the morphine could hide that pain.

I can't believe how many times I've looked death in the eye, but I'm still here, and I've learned to make time to express my true feelings. Especially to my loved ones, because I just don't know when our last day will be. No one does; all it takes is texting "see you soon," while driving, and never seeing that person again.

OVERALL, camp life was laid back, but I didn't like switching bunkies, and it happened regularly because inmates came and left weekly. There was some good in this, though, because everyone I met taught me something. It just came down to whether they were a blessing or a lesson.

One of my bunkies was named Ked. He was almost seventy years old, self-made, on the board of the Harvard Parents Fund, and the type of guy you'd see sharing a laugh with a politician at the greenest country club in town. He'd been sentenced to ten years and ordered to pay around $22 million in restitution for violating federal securities laws. The media painted him as a con man and a people pleaser, although he said there was more to the story, and that his childhood wasn't as rosy as his champagne toasts at the Four Seasons Hotel. He said his father had abandoned him and his mother when he was eight, and then, fueled by disappointment, he was forever determined to prove to his father that he'd be a success at any cost.

Like me, it seemed Ked had a void to fill. And even though I didn't approve of his crime, I liked him, because he was smart. So much so that I sought his knowledge and wisdom, and created a business arrangement with him in order to obtain any of it that I could. Our agreement was simple: In exchange for his mentorship, I'd keep our bunk area organized and give it one deep clean per week. His mentorship would be dispensed spontaneously in small doses when he wasn't reading financial news, jumping rope, or doing pilates.

ONE AFTERNOON, I was gazing over the partition of our cell at all the inmates patiently waiting for security clearance to attend the mess hall. We were in lockdown because the Boston Marathon bomber was being securely deposited into our main prison for medical attention.

Ked caught my ear when he said, "Eric, don't get lost trying to fit in with these guys. Focus on yourself."

I looked down toward Ked, lying back on his bottom bunk, with his reading glasses on, flipping through the *Wall Street Journal*, and replied: "I hear you."

Ked rested the newspaper across his chest and looked up at me, deep in thought, and said, "Most of these guys who are running around in their posses are weak. They're afraid to be alone. If you look closely, you'll notice that most people who run around in big circles are afraid to be alone." Ked paused, adding: "If there's one thing you remember from being trapped in this place, remember this . . . being alone is good. It gives you time to think."

I thought for a moment, agreeing with Ked, and replied with a smile: "Maybe I should thank my mom for locking me in my room."

Ked laughed and said, "You should. Being alone probably helped you work through a lot of problems. Most people don't get this. They think money will fix all their problems. What they don't understand is that money won't fix a broken mindset, which is a problem, because your life's only as good as your mindset."

I agreed with Ked again, knowing that for years I'd thought money would solve all my problems, and it did solve some, but never as many as I solved while being alone and in control of my own thoughts. I proved this throughout my next several months of alone time in prison.

I deduced through a series of experiments that when I felt shitty, it wasn't because of my circumstances; it was because my negative thoughts had created those shitty circumstances. Any time I had a negative thought, I could literally feel it eating away at me from the inside out. In contrast, when I had a positive thought, I could feel it healing me.

I was amazed by how powerful my thoughts were. I was amazed by how powerful thoughts were in general. They had literally created every single man-made thing around me. The steel locker, the jumpsuit, the towel, the notebook, the pencil, the window, the concrete . . . all of it, it was all created by thoughts. Every single man-made thing in the entire world was created by thoughts. Everything started with a thought before it ever physically existed. That's some serious power, and exactly why I couldn't fathom ever having a negative thought again, even secretly, toward distant enemies. That would only sabotage me.

In order to become "the one," I needed to think about what I wanted, rather than what I didn't want. My thoughts were the most powerful thing I had. They're the most powerful thing everyone has. And what we think about is our choice. It's called free will.

34

VALIDATION

After sitting in the camp for about a year, waiting for news, Dave notified me that my appeal had been denied in the Second Circuit. But a lot can change in a year, and Ron wanted me out of prison immediately. I think it was a gift to me, because his days were numbered, as he was dying of cancer. And sure enough, Dave came to visit me with the news that, at Ron's recommendation, the prosecutor had filed a motion requesting the court reduce my original sentence. Unfortunately, it wasn't that easy. I still had to be transported back to Albany so I could stand before Judge Sharpe, in hopes he'd shorten my time.

I wasn't excited for transport, but prisoners are constantly moved between different prisons and jails as their security levels change, and as population management issues are dealt with. They're also moved when they need to appear in court, and now that I had a scheduled appearance in the Albany Federal Courthouse, there was only one way to get me there—diesel therapy —a process when prisoners are shackled and transported via bus or plane to their new destination, while stopping at multiple prisons along the way for extended periods of time. It can last several days or several weeks, and inmates are never given information regarding their next destination or what day they'll be moved. It's a security measure implemented by the Bureau of Prisons to prevent prisoners from escaping.

The diesel bus I was transported on contained about a dozen prisoners, many of whom were sentenced to life without parole. I didn't speak with them or the two armed guards—I just sat with my waist chain on, looking through the tiny holes of the metal screen covering my window.

It was the first time I'd been in civilization in over a year, and as we passed through traffic, I stared down at all the law-abiding citizens in their cars. They looked tired, which was disappointing because I'd just spent over a year reinventing myself and was excited to experience freedom with them. It looked like they needed a hug and to be told everything was going to be okay. Many looked controlled by consumerism. I could see the stress in their faces. I wished I had a megaphone, right then and there, to remind them consumerism is perpetuated by brilliant marketers who rewire our hearts so we'll give them our hard-earned money. I wanted them to understand that marketers are trained to know what we all want and what we'll all pay for, and that's love, security, and recognition. Why? Because they're the three things that are behind everything we do in life, and I mean everything.

Whether we know it or not, subconsciously we all wake up and go about our day in search of love, security, and recognition. We're like robots, on autopilot, trying to capture these things. Just think, every person you know, including yourself, is seeking at least one of these things right now. This is a fact, and it's important to know that love, security, and recognition are three of the main drivers in everyone's life. And they're valid drivers, which need to be embraced, because they motivate us. However, it's important to understand that these motivators also cause us stress, which is something that we all have and must actively manage.

Stress isn't something you should fear, though, because having a small amount of it is good. In fact, it's necessary for evolution; it keeps us growing. It's just the gap between where we are and where we want to be. My problem was, as a child, I always wanted more friends, more money, and more toys. And as I grew up, those same wants and desires continued to grow with me, causing me an enormous amount of stress, because as I grew, my goals didn't change. For example, at the age of thirty, I still thought that if I had more friends, more money, and more toys, the better life would be. But I learned the hard way this couldn't be further from the truth. I learned, because I can now see how I was held hostage by my childhood cravings—for years. I was a slave to the "American dream." I was so focused on getting more and doing more that I didn't have time to feel or enjoy all that I already had. I was lost in search of validation from people I didn't even know.

I wasn't the only one who was lost in search of external validation. I knew a lot of people who bought into the newest trends, simply to be noticed and accepted, and in the process, were creating mountains of debt that were dragging them to their grave. It may be difficult for some to admit this, but it's true. Many of us buy a lot of shit just to be noticed and accepted by the popular or dominant group. At least, I did. I can't believe how many designer labels I had bought that I didn't even have time to use. Labels that took up space. Space to be free. Space to grow into my true self. Fuck, I spent millions trying to be someone I was told to be, and it became an exhausting undertaking. I wish I'd had an instruction manual for life. It could have just said: Be loved for who you are, not for who you're told to be.

I'm embarrassed by how many years I spent keeping up with

the newest trends, just to fit in. What a waste. I still do it a little, but at least now I'm aware of it and I manage it. I do it when I need to go to a formal event or a business function, but I balance out that road show with remote vacations where I can walk barefoot. The question is: Why do some of us post pictures of our vacations? I know why, though; it's because we're seeking connection. It's because we can't make it through this life alone. No one can. That's why we're always looking for more connections. The key is to find ones that feel right, because our external relationships are constantly shaping our internal world.

35

VISUALIZATION

After a month of diesel therapy, I stood before Judge Sharpe in my orange jumpsuit and shackles. Since I only had a few months remaining on my sentence, he graciously gave me time served so I could go back out into the world and say, "Vera, what's for dinner?" And sure enough, after receiving a couple surprise letters from her while in prison, she was waiting for me with a stocked fridge and a fresh set of sheets.

I had envisioned Vera would be there for me when I was set free, because by now, I knew exactly how to get what I wanted in life. It was through visualization, which was simply about creating visions of the things I wanted to appear in my life, and then using those visions to control my thoughts. I'd then take those thoughts and develop plans around them. I'd then back those plans with patience, persistence, and faith, which was simply about putting the work in, believing in myself, and then letting the universe take control. This is how I got everything I wanted in life. It's how I went from the bottom to the top. It's how I met the woman of my dreams. It's how I made enough money so I'd never have to worry about where my next meal was going to come from. I did it all by taking control of my thoughts, because I innately knew everything in my life was a reflection of my thoughts.

What I'm saying is that the law of attraction really works. Seriously, I had literally spent years alone, as a kid, cutting out pictures in magazines that depicted all the things I wanted, and all the things I wanted to do in life. I would even carry on imaginary conversations with the type of people I wanted to meet someday, on my solo walks to school, while kicking stones down the road. Shit, I'd even slap high-fives to people who didn't exist. And after years of living in my imaginary world, I can finally see how my thoughts spiraled into my reality.

ACKNOWLEDGMENTS

I'd like to thank all my customers and suppliers from the past for our endless handshake deals without a contract. Without you, I wouldn't have made it.

QR CODE